WINE Administrator's Handbook

WINE
Administrator's
Handbook

Michele Petrovsky and Tom Parkinson

M&T Books
An imprint of IDG Books Worldwide, Inc.
Foster City, CA ■ Chicago, IL ■ Indianapolis, IN ■ New York, NY

WINE Administrator's Handbook

Published by
M&T Books
An imprint of IDG Books Worldwide, Inc.
919 E. Hillsdale Blvd., Suite 400
Foster City, CA 94404
www.idgbooks.com (IDG Books Worldwide Web site)

Larry Ewing (lewing@isc.tamu.edu) using the GIMP (www.gimp.org/), and was subsequently modified for use by IDG Books Worldwide on this book's cover by Tuomas Kuosmanen (tiger@gimp.org). Tuomas also used the GIMP for his work with Tux.

ISBN: 0-7645-4630-9

Printed in the United States of America

10 9 8 7 6 5 4 3 2 1

1O/RX/QT/QQ/FC

Distributed in the United States by IDG Books Worldwide, Inc.

Distributed by CDG Books Canada Inc. for Canada; by Transworld Publishers Limited in the United Kingdom; by IDG Norge Books for Norway; by IDG Sweden Books for Sweden; by IDG Books Australia Publishing Corporation Pty. Ltd. for Australia and New Zealand; by TransQuest Publishers Pte Ltd. for Singapore, Malaysia, Thailand, Indonesia, and Hong Kong; by Gotop Information Inc. for Taiwan; by ICG Muse, Inc. for Japan; by Intersoft for South Africa; by Eyrolles for France; by International Thomson Publishing for Germany, Austria and Switzerland; by Distribuidora Cuspide for Argentina; by LR International for Brazil; by Galileo Libros for Chile; by Ediciones ZETA S.C.R. Ltda. for Peru; by WS Computer Publishing Corporation, Inc., for the Philippines; by Contemporanea de Ediciones for Venezuela; by Express Computer Distributors for the Caribbean and West Indies; by Micronesia Media Distributor, Inc. for Micronesia; by Chips Computadoras S.A. de C.V. for Mexico; by Editorial Norma de Panama S.A. for Panama; by American Bookshops for Finland.

For general information on IDG Books Worldwide's books in the U.S., please call our Consumer Customer Service department at 800-762-2974. For reseller information, including discounts and premium sales, please call our Reseller Customer Service department at 800-434-3422.

For information on where to purchase IDG Books Worldwide's books outside the U.S., please contact our International Sales department at 317-596-5530 or fax 317-596-5692.

For consumer information on foreign language translations, please contact our Customer Service department at 800-434-3422, fax 317-596-5692, or e-mail rights@idgbooks.com.

For information on licensing foreign or domestic rights, please phone +1-650-655-3109.

For sales inquiries and special prices for bulk quantities, please contact our Sales department at 650-655-3200 or write to the address above.

For information on using IDG Books Worldwide's books in the classroom or for ordering examination copies, please contact our Educational Sales department at 800-434-2086 or fax 317-596-5499.

For press review copies, author interviews, or other publicity information, please contact our Public Relations department at 650-655-3000 or fax 650-655-3299.

For authorization to photocopy items for corporate, personal, or educational use, please contact Copyright Clearance Center, 222 Rosewood Drive, Danvers, MA 01923, or fax 978-750-4470.

Library of Congress Cataloging-in-Publication Data

Petrovsky, Michele

Wine administrator's handbook/Michele Petrovsky and Tom Parkinson.

p. cm.

ISBN 0-7645-4630-9 (alk. paper)

1. Windows (Computer file) 2. Wine (Computer file) 3. UNIX (Computer file) I. Parkinson, Tom (Tom Edward Joseph) II. Title

QA76.76.O63 P5289 2000

005.4'469--dc21   00-022389

 is a registered trademark or trademark under exclusive license to IDG Books Worldwide, Inc. from International Data Group, Inc. in the United States and/or other countries.

 is a registered trademark of IDG Books Worldwide, Inc.,

ABOUT IDG BOOKS WORLDWIDE

Welcome to the world of IDG Books Worldwide.

IDG Books Worldwide, Inc., is a subsidiary of International Data Group, the world's largest publisher of computer-related information and the leading global provider of information services on information technology. IDG was founded more than 30 years ago by Patrick J. McGovern and now employs more than 9,000 people worldwide. IDG publishes more than 290 computer publications in over 75 countries. More than 90 million people read one or more IDG publications each month.

Launched in 1990, IDG Books Worldwide is today the #1 publisher of best-selling computer books in the United States. We are proud to have received eight awards from the Computer Press Association in recognition of editorial excellence and three from Computer Currents' First Annual Readers' Choice Awards. Our best-selling ...For Dummies® series has more than 50 million copies in print with translations in 31 languages. IDG Books Worldwide, through a joint venture with IDG's Hi-Tech Beijing, became the first U.S. publisher to publish a computer book in the People's Republic of China. In record time, IDG Books Worldwide has become the first choice for millions of readers around the world who want to learn how to better manage their businesses.

Our mission is simple: Every one of our books is designed to bring extra value and skill-building instructions to the reader. Our books are written by experts who understand and care about our readers. The knowledge base of our editorial staff comes from years of experience in publishing, education, and journalism — experience we use to produce books to carry us into the new millennium. In short, we care about books, so we attract the best people. We devote special attention to details such as audience, interior design, use of icons, and illustrations. And because we use an efficient process of authoring, editing, and desktop publishing our books electronically, we can spend more time ensuring superior content and less time on the technicalities of making books.

You can count on our commitment to deliver high-quality books at competitive prices on topics you want to read about. At IDG Books Worldwide, we continue in the IDG tradition of delivering quality for more than 30 years. You'll find no better book on a subject than one from IDG Books Worldwide.

John J. Kilcullen

John Kilcullen
Chairman and CEO
IDG Books Worldwide, Inc.

WINNER

*Eighth Annual
Computer Press
Awards ≧1992*

IX WINNER

*Ninth Annual
Computer Press
Awards ≧1993*

X WINNER

*Tenth Annual
Computer Press
Awards ≧1994*

XI WINNER

*Eleventh Annual
Computer Press
Awards ≧1995*

IDG is the world's leading IT media, research and exposition company. Founded in 1964, IDG had 1997 revenues of $2.05 billion and has more than 9,000 employees worldwide. IDG offers the widest range of media options that reach IT buyers in 75 countries representing 95% of worldwide IT spending. IDG's diverse product and services portfolio spans six key areas including print publishing, online publishing, expositions and conferences, market research, education and training, and global marketing services. More than 90 million people read one or more of IDG's 290 magazines and newspapers, including IDG's leading global brands — Computerworld, PC World, Network World, Macworld and the Channel World family of publications. IDG Books Worldwide is one of the fastest-growing computer book publishers in the world, with more than 700 titles in 36 languages. The "...For Dummies®" series alone has more than 50 million copies in print. IDG offers online users the largest network of technology-specific Web sites around the world through IDG.net (http://www.idg.net), which comprises more than 225 targeted Web sites in 55 countries worldwide. International Data Corporation (IDC) is the world's largest provider of information technology data, analysis and consulting, with research centers in over 41 countries and more than 400 research analysts worldwide. IDG World Expo is a leading producer of more than 168 globally branded conferences and expositions in 35 countries including E3 (Electronic Entertainment Expo), Macworld Expo, ComNet, Windows World Expo, ICE (Internet Commerce Expo), Agenda, DEMO, and Spotlight. IDG's training subsidiary, ExecuTrain, is the world's largest computer training company, with more than 230 locations worldwide and 785 training courses. IDG Marketing Services helps industry-leading IT companies build international brand recognition by developing global integrated marketing programs via IDG's print, online and exposition products worldwide. Further information about the company can be found at www.idg.com.   1/26/00

Credits

Acquisitions Editor
Laura Lewin

Development Editor
Eric Newman

Technical Editor
Marcus Meissner

Copy Editor
S.B. Kleinman

Project Coordinators
Linda Marousek
Marcos Vergara

Quality Control Specialists
Laura Taflinger
Chris Weisbart

Graphics and Production Specialists
Robert Bihlmayer
Jude Levinson
Ramses Ramirez
Victor Pérez-Varela
Dina F Quan

Book Designer
Kurt Krames

Proofreading and Indexing
York Production Services

Cover Illustration
Larry Wilson

About the Authors

Michele Petrovsky holds a master of science in Computer and Information Science from the University of Pittsburgh. Michele has administered Unix and Linux systems and networks, has programmed at the application level in everything from C to 4GLs, has worked as a technical editor and writer for a number of years, and has taught at the community college and university levels. Michele is currently an assistant professor with the Information Technology Department of Mount Saint Vincent University in Halifax, Nova Scotia, and welcomes conversations with readers at `m.petrovsky@ns.sympatico.ca`.

Tom Parkinson's dual background in Library Science and Computer/Information Science as well as his nearly two decades' experience in implementing and managing specialized applications in heterogeneous environments make him ideally suited to researching and writing on a topic such as WINE. You can talk to Tom at `tparkins@dcccnet.dccc.edu`.

We dedicate this book to our friends at The Gathering Place and The Navajo Co-op, both of which seek to showcase the work of Native American artists and provide literacy and health programs, conducted by local women, to residents of the Navajo Nation and surrounding regions.

Like the WINE Project, The Gathering Place and The Navajo Co-op seek to build the future on a firm foundation. Both groups' efforts will enrich not only one community but our entire society.

To learn more about The Gathering Place, The Navajo Co-op, and their programs, visit this URL: www.cia-g.com/~gathplac/index.htm.

We think you'll be as impressed with these folks and their work as we were.

Preface

This brief introduction acquaints you with:

- the WINE Project
- what *WINE Administrator's Handbook* contains
- who can benefit from reading it
- what the book asks of its readers
- how the book is organized, and what its sections offer
- what the book means when it uses certain symbols and styles
- the most effective way to use the book

The WINE Project

WINE has been called a Windows compatibility layer. It allows applications that rely on the Windows 3.*x* and Win32 APIs to run seamlessly under Intel Unix and X Window. Further, WINE offers not only a program loader that permits unmodified 16- or 32-bit binaries to execute but also a development toolkit called Winelib that allows developers to port Windows-based application source to PC-based Unix. WINE supports most widely used versions of PC Unix, such as Linux, FreeBSD, and Solaris.

WINE does not require Microsoft Windows. Rather, WINE is a completely alternative implementation of the specifications upon which Microsoft built its various Windows interfaces. As its developers put it, WINE's source code is *completely Microsoft-free*. Nonetheless, WINE can work with native system DLLs in some cases.

WINE can be downloaded from the WINE Project's web site at www.winehq.com as:

- complete source code, with accompanying documentation and examples
- precompiled executables

The suite is freely redistributable, under licensing terms similar to those of BSD Unix.

WINE at a Glance

WINE's many impressive features include:

- 16- and 32-bit x86 code
- advanced thunking capabilities
- binary compatibility
- graphics
  - internal PostScript driver printing interface
  - metafile driver
  - partial DirectX support for games
  - remote display to any X terminal
  - full support for GDI and many of the new features of GDI32
  - support for native Win16 printer drivers
  - X11-based graphics display
- large interrupt library for programs using real-mode interrupt calls
- multimedia and data communications
  - ASPI Scanner support
  - support for sound, as well as for alternative input devices
  - support for a variety of modems and other serial devices
  - Winsock TCP/IP networking
- optional use of third-party DLLs
- reverse-engineering that assures *bug-for-bug* compatibility
- support for loading DOS, Windows 3.*x* and Win32 binaries
- support for Win16 and Win32 function calls
- WINE API
  - 32-bit resource compiler
  - automatically generated API documentation
  - built-in debugger and configurable trace messages
  - designed for source compatibility with Win32 code
  - internationalization, with support for 16 languages

WINE's Status

At the time this book was being written, WINE contained more than 350,000 lines of C code, written by well over 100 people from all over the world. Their product implements more than 90 percent of the system calls outlined in Windows specifications such as ECMA-234 and Open32.

However, you should be aware that, even now, WINE is still very much under development. The members of the WINE Project consider their suite still in alpha or early beta condition, and not suitable for use in a production environment. Despite these limitations, though, WINE has proven useful in providing interoperability with Intel Unix for a wide variety of Windows programs. Further, WINE's developers expect the suite to be fully debugged and functional by late 2000.

What's in This Book

WINE Administrator's Handbook is just that — a volume that can be used by anyone who must obtain, install, configure, manage, or troubleshoot WINE. It presents real-world guidelines, examples, and tips for doing all of those things. What's more, it discusses these techniques in the context of several of the operating system platforms under which WINE can run. Finally, the book extends its coverage to other tools with which WINE can cooperate to provide full interoperability in heterogeneous environments. In this last category, the book emphasizes using Samba to offer Windows– and Intel Unix–based machines the ability to share one another's resources seamlessly.

Who Should Read This Book

System analysts, system administrators, and even managers whose responsibility it is to decide upon new software tools can all benefit from reading *WINE Administrator's Handbook*. We have not, however, incorporated information that we consider of value primarily or solely to developers.

What's Needed to Understand the Book

The handbook does not introduce the reader to the basics of Intel Unix. Rather, it assumes that he or she understands how Unix in general, and Linux in particular, handles such things as:

- command aliases
- configuration files
- file access permissions
- file ownership
- hierarchical file systems
- running processes in background
- scheduling jobs
- techniques such as input and output redirection, and pipes
- updating files
- user IDs and passwords
- virtual memory

On the other hand, because many of the book's readers may have a basic grasp of Intel Unix but may not have worked with it extensively, the book begins by presenting requirements and instructions for installing the most popular commercial versions of Linux.

How the Book Is Structured

The body of *WINE Administrator's Handbook* devotes one chapter to each of the topics an administrator is most likely to have to address. What's more, these subjects are covered in the order in which that administrator is most likely to encounter them:

- system requirements and preparation
- downloading, installing, and configuring
- providing interoperability in heterogeneous environments through partnership with Samba
- troubleshooting in standalone and networked environments
- recognizing applications' performance records under WINE

Conventions

This book uses some special conventions that make the material easier to follow and understand:

- Key combinations such as Ctrl+Alt+Delete are joined by plus signs.
- Menu choices use a notation like Start ➪ Run, which means press the Start button, and then choose Run from the new menu that appears.
- *Italic text* indicates new terms or placeholders, and is sometimes used for emphasis.
- **Bold text** indicates text you type.
- `Monotype text` indicates code, onscreen text, or Internet addresses.

In addition, two icons used throughout the book help you identify specific pieces of information to which you should pay particular attention:

Tip

Tips address significant performance issues.

Caution

Cautions alert you to situations that might result in system failure.

How to Use the Book Efficiently

Those of you unfamiliar with working with preliminary versions of software, or with Linux GUIs, might want to begin at the end of the handbook, getting a conceptual framework for working with WINE from Appendix A and its discussion of the software standards upon which WINE rests. On the other hand, the more experienced system managers among you can dive right in at Chapter 1 to begin gathering nuts-and-bolts information on implementing WINE.

In either case, the book's structure, which isolates each significant aspect of that implementation to its own chapter, is itself a tool in the efficient use of the handbook.

Sources

The documentation upon which we drew in preparing this book, like WINE itself, follows an Open Source philosophy. In keeping with that philosophy, we present here a list of the Web sites to which we referred.

- http://kerkis.math.aegean.gr/~dspin/pubs/jrnl/1997-CSI-WinAPI/html/win.html

- http://www.about.com (©1999 by Aron Hsiao, licensed to About.com. Used by permission of About.com, which can be found on the Web at www.about.com. All rights reserved)

- http://www.calderasystems.com

- http://www.freebsd.org

- http://www.linux.com

- http://www.redhat.com

- http://www.samba.org

- http://www.suse.com

- http://www.winehq.com

Acknowledgments

No matter how many names are on or inside the cover of a book, be assured that all those who contributed to it have not been mentioned. So we'd like to take this opportunity to recognize the work of some of the "unsung heroes" of this volume. Many members of the WINE Project, including Alexandre Julliard, Ove Kaaven, Paul Merrell, Doug Ridgway, James Sutherland, and Ulrich Weigand, were kind enough to respond quickly and fully to our many e-mail inquiries. Their efforts aided ours enormously.

Contents at a Glance

Contents

Part I

Installation and Configuration

Hard drive

PC-based UNIX can talk to any size hard drive a PC's own BIOS can talk to. Even so, we must still mention two points regarding hard drives: controllers and space available.

Hard drive controllers Intel UNIX supports hard drive controllers including IDE, EIDE, and SCSI. If you anticipate implementing WINE on an older PC, and therefore probably on one that uses an IDE controller, bear in mind that many such controllers can support two drives. This feature, then, gives you a means of dealing with the size limitations of many IDE drives, enabling you to isolate OS and WINE to one such, leaving the other completely available to the Microsoft applications that WINE will render.

EIDE drives, on the other hand, are unlikely to present you with the space limitations of their IDE predecessors. Such drives, assuming they contain enough free space for the OS, WINE, and the apps it supports, add no real complications to WINE's implementation.

The same can be said for SCSI drives. For example, if you use any of the SCSI controllers listed in Table 1-2, you should have no problems installing any Intel UNIX, or WINE, to the related drive.

Table 1-2 *A Small Sampling of SCSI Controllers Supported by PC-Based UNIX*

These Models	From This Manufacturer	Support This Bus	And Are Supported by These OSes
AHA-152x, AHA-154x, AHA-174x, and AHA-274x	Adaptec	ISA, ISA, EISA, and VLB	All the Adaptec controllers mentioned are supported by all of, Caldera OpenLinux, RedHat Linux, SCO UnixWare, and Sun Microsystems Solaris
ST-01 and ST-02	Seagate	ISA	Both these Seagate cards are supported by both Caldera OpenLinux and RedHat Linux
T128 and T228	Trantor	ISA	Both these Trantor cards are supported by both Caldera OpenLinux and RedHat Linux

Tip

In addition to the SCSI controllers outlined in Table 1-2, there are dozens of others, from a variety of manufacturers, that coexist quite easily with most Intel UNIX versions. If you plan to use SCSI as part of your WINE implementation, check the documentation for your operating system to find alternatives to the cards noted in the table.

Available drive space To support a full installation of PC-based UNIX, count on needing at least 400MB of free disk space *for the OS and X Window alone.* And remember, this is a minimum, *and* does not take into account the space WINE and any applications the latter supports might require.

While a binaries-only WINE installation — that is, the suite without any applications running under it — requires as little as 5MB free disk, anyone anticipating recompiling WINE should provide at least another 200MB. Furthermore, should you plan to run applications under WINE that might need large amounts of swap space, or should your operating system implementation include features beyond the basic, this ballpark subtotal of about 600MB could rise significantly.

Diskette drive

If the system to which you plan to add WINE and its PC UNIX platform meets the operating system's requirements for BIOS, that system's diskette drive will by definition also be accessible by WINE's underlying OS. But you're not quite out of the woods on this point yet. Bear in mind that, if you must install and configure WINE's operating system as well as WINE itself, you may have to boot from a diskette as part of the former installation. Therefore, your intended platform should offer either

- A 5.25-inch, 1.2MB, or
- A 3.5-inch, 1.44MB diskette drive.

CD-ROM drive

First, the good news. Since PC-based UNIX can work with such a wide variety of SCSI controllers, it can support any CD-ROM drive that can be attached to such a card. Now, even better news. Most Intel UNIX versions support *all* EIDE CD-ROM controllers.

This fortunate combination produces the selection of CD drives outlined in Table 1-3.

Table 1-3 *Some CD-ROM Drives Supported by PC-Based UNIX*

Manufacturer	Model
Creative Labs	CD200
GoldStar	R420
LMS Phillips	CM206
Mitsumi	FX001D
Sony	Several drives in the CDUx series
Teac	CD-55A

Tape drive

Tape drives, while not as common to PCs as to larger computers, must still be taken into account as you prepare to implement WINE and any of its OS platforms. Most varieties of Intel UNIX support SCSI tape drives from such manufacturers as

- Colorado
- Exabyte
- Quantum
- Sony

Be sure to check your drive's documentation. Intel UNIX ignores not only non-SCSI tape drives, as you can see from the abbreviated list above, but also drives that connect through the parallel port.

Printer

Like most operating systems, PC UNIX supports all common parallel printers. Serial printers, on the other hand, fare poorly under these OSes. Expect significant difficulties in trying to identify a serial printer to WINE's system platform. However, once identification is successful, expect WINE to handle smoothly these or any printers that are correctly configured.

Monitor

As is the case in the Microsoft OS universe, Intel UNIX supports any monitor that can operate in *Video Graphics Array (VGA) or Super Video Graphics Array (SVGA)* modes. This capability alone, however, doesn't ensure that X Window and WINE will experience no display disruptions. Be sure that your monitor can interact with *all* resolutions of which the adapter controlling it is capable.

Video adapter

Once again as in the Microsoft world, PC-based UNIX decides whether or not to support a video adapter based primarily on that card's chip set. XFree86, the version of X Window supplied with most versions of Intel UNIX, can work with the adapters outlined in Table 1-4, among others.

Table 1-4 *Selected Video Adapters Supported by PC UNIX*

Adapter	Video Host(s) Supported
Cirrus Logic GD542x	XF86_SVGA
Cirrus Logic GD543x	XF86_SVGA
Creative Blaster Exxtreme	XF86_SVGA
Creative Labs Graphics Blaster MA201	XF86_SVGA
Diamond Fire GL 1000	XF86_3Dlabs
Diamond SpeedStar 24	XF86_SVGA
Diamond Stealth 64 VRAM	XF86_S3
Genoa Phantom 64i with S3 SDAC	XF86_S3
Hercules Graphite Pro	XF86_AGX
Trident TVGA 8800CS	XF86_VGA16

Tip

Table 1-4 covers only a few percent of the video adapters with which PC Unix will work. For the most complete list, go to http://www.xfree86.org/cardlist.txt.

Audio adapter

While PC UNIX supports many common sound cards, it can sometimes have more problems configuring these components than in setting up other devices. Check your operating system documentation in order to ensure the audio adapter is supported by the operating system. Also be sure of the details of the way in which the sound card must be configured.

 Tip

Even some fully Sound Blaster–compatible cards may not work with some Intel UNIX versions. If your audio adapter uses an ASP chip set, or offers specialized MIDI effects, it may present problems to the OS.

WINE

The fact that WINE was and is very much a work in progress introduces some idiosyncrasies to its OS compatibility profile. Therefore, in this section, we'll examine WINE's operating system requirements more closely. In addition, we'll look at the suite's disk-space needs.

Kernel versions

In theory, WINE can run under all but the oldest Linux kernel versions. However, many of its newest features and bug fixes were developed under Linux kernels in the 2.0.*x* series. So, you may need to upgrade your OS in order to get full WINE functionality. In short, assume that WINE requires a Linux kernel version later than 2.0.

Libraries

Not only does WINE require several libraries, it may require different ones under different operating system platforms. We've summarized WINE's library and other supporting software requirements in Table 1-5

Table 1-5 *WINE's Supporting Software Requirements*

These features	Are needed to	by this OS
bison, flex	Compile WINE	All versions of Linux
clone(2) system call	Run WINE	All versions of Linux beginning with 2.0
GCC 2.7 or later	Compile WINE	All versions of Linux
GNU toolchain (i.e., GCC, GAS, etc.)	Compile WINE	Solaris 7.x
libc6 (glibc2)	Support multithreading	All versions of Linux
libXpm	Support X-Windows	All versions of Linux
X11 development libraries and related header files	Compile WINE	All versions of Linux

Multithreading

WINE must work with reentrant X libraries if it is to support multi-threaded applications. In order to ensure the presence of this trait, your operating system must either

- Have been installed and configured to include the libc6 library
- Have had its X libraries manually compiled

Tip

All versions of Linux released in 1999 satisfy these points by default.

X Window managers

While 32-bit Windows OSes do offer character-mode operation, WINE itself, even in presenting such console windows, requires X Window. However, the suite has no other requirements in this area. WINE uses standard X libraries, so no additional ones need be loaded.

However, WINE can use either

- Its own window management, or
- An external window manager, specified at the command line by means of the -managed option

In the first instance, WINE's windows will resemble those of Windows 3.1 or Windows 95, depending on how you've handled other, related configuration options. In the latter case, WINE will use the standard X11 window manager.

File systems

WINE, as file-system independent as it is window-manager transparent, will work with any file system its operating system platform supports. Table 1-6 presents some of these.

Table 1-6 *File Systems and Intel UNIX*

This Operating System	Can Recognize and Access These File Systems
OpenLinux 2.2 and higher	NTFS, Windows 98 FAT32, Windows 95 FAT32, FAT16
Red Hat 5.1 and higher	Windows 98 FAT32, Windows 95 FAT32, FAT16
Solaris 7	Windows 98 FAT32, Windows 95 FAT32, FAT16
UnixWare 7	Windows 98 FAT32, Windows 95 FAT32, FAT16

Available disk space

To house (and if need be) compile WINE, you'll need

- About 130MB free disk space
- An additional 20MB in the /tmp directory, for WINE's interim files

What's more, since WINE's default home on your system will be the **/usr** file subsystem, this free space should be available there. To verify that it is, use a **df** (*disk free*) command like this.

```
df /usr
```

RAM and swap

WINE's designers recommend a minimum of 32MB RAM, and the same amount of swap space, on any PC intended to run WINE. Software developers and any other users who might modify and debug or recompile WINE's source, however, should anticipate that any amounts of RAM and swap space less than 64MB will result in poor performance.

Preparing for Specific Operating Systems

In this section, we'll discuss, not factors that permit WINE's installing and running, but rather

- Incompatibilities that some of WINE's operating system platforms might experience, and which might prevent or at least complicate the suite's implementation
- Features of those platforms with which WINE may have to compete for system resources

The Caldera environment

Its entirely GUI-driven installation, reliance on the Linux 2.2 kernel, and use of the KDE desktop manager to offer a familiar, Windows 9x–like interface are some of the most notable features of Caldera OpenLinux 2.2. Both the implementation of the newest Linux kernel, and OpenLinux 2.2's larger-than-usual-with-Linux reliance on a graphical interface, however, present possible problem areas to WINE.

Several features of the 2.2 kernel have special relevance to any potential WINE platform, and particularly to platforms that play departmental or enterprise server roles. For instance, this most recent kernel

- Can read, although not reliably write to, NTFS drives
- Fully supports Windows 98 FAT 32 drives in addition to the FAT 16 drives detected even by earlier versions of Linux
- Supports up to 16 CPUs in Symmetric Multiprocessing (SMP) schemes
- Supports, and improves upon the efforts made by earlier versions of Linux for, extending file systems across multiple disks, thereby also permitting using RAID levels 0, 1, 4, and 5

Such abilities, coupled with other OpenLinux 2.2 features like

- Administrative tools from the mundane (BRU backup and restore) to the advanced (IP firewall and accounting utilities)
- BootMagic

- Client-related services such as DHCP, Samba, DNS, Telnet, FTP, Netscape communicator, Apache, Sendmail, News, and Majordomo
- PartitionMagic Caldera Edition
- Protocols including, TCP/IP, Ethernet, PPP, SLIP, UUCP, SMTP, POP, IMAP, NFS, SMB, and IPX
- WordPerfect 8 personal edition

make OpenLinux more than viable in the department or enterprise, but also make its demands on system resources more extensive. Table 1-7 outlines some of these requirements.

Table 1-7 *System Requirements for Caldera OpenLinux 2.2*

This Feature	Requires a Minimum of	But Works Even Better With
CPU	x386	Pentium, Pentium II, or Pentium Pro
RAM	32MB	64MB
Swap (note that swap space should, ideally, equal the amount of RAM, but cannot exceed 128MB)	32MB	64MB
Free disk	300MB (for a minimal OS installation)	low-volume systems: 160MB; standard recommendation: 580MB; recommended for commercial systems: 780MB (provides for the addition of StarOffice 5, WordPerfect 8, BRU 15.0, and Communicator 4.51); recommended for full installations and/or departmental or higher-level servers: 1.2GB

The Red Hat environment

Considered by many the market leader and de facto standard for PC-based UNIX, Red Hat Linux 5.1 also played an important role in the development of this book. We used Red Hat as the first OS under which WINE was installed and banged on. In the process, we discovered only one area in which Red Hat might present possible problems to WINE.

Red Hat's Web site (`www.redhat.com`) presents very extensive lists of compatible hardware. Further, it points out specific components that are *incompatible*. However, the Red Hat site doesn't fully follow through. In several critical categories such as CPU, controllers, disk drives, and SCSI adapters, it distinguishes, but doesn't immediately explain, separate levels of support:

- Devices that are not only fully compatible but also fully supported
- Devices that are fully compatible but only partially supported
- Devices that are compatible but not supported

A bit more browsing of Red Hat's online support center, however, elicited a clarification of these categories. Table 1-8 summarizes.

Table 1-8 *Red Hat Linux and Hardware Devices*

This Category	Called This by Red Hat	Means This to the User	And May Present These Problems to the OS and WINE
devices that are not only fully compatible but also fully supported	Tier 1 Supported Hardware	hardware that the kernel can easily detect and use; i.e., known by Red Hat to be reliable	none
devices that are fully compatible but only partially supported	Tier 2 Supported Hardware	hardware that should be detectable by and usable with the kernel	inappropriate interaction with other hardware
devices that are compatible but not supported	Compatible but Unsupported Hardware	hardware that should be detectable and usable by the kernel in some configurations	lack of availability from Red Hat of drivers for such devices; no support from Red Hat for third-party drivers for such devices
incompatible devices	Incompatible Hardware	hardware known by Red Hat to be incompatible with Red Hat	no support from Red Hat or any drivers you might find for such devices

Luckily, our initial Linux/WINE platform's hardware all fell into Tier 1. But such caution on Red Hat's part suggests the need for caution on yours, to ensure as smooth an OS and WINE install as we experienced. Check Red Hat's online hardware compatibility information carefully. You'll find it at `www.redhat.com/support/docs/rhl/intel/ rh52-hardware-intel-3.html`.

The Sun environment

In its Intel-based incarnations, Solaris 7 resembles Red Hat Linux in the varying degrees of ease with which it can support hardware devices. But be careful: some high-end versions of this system, such as its Enterprise and ISP server packages, require patching the OS in a number of areas, and as much as 4GB drive space, 256MB RAM, and 1GB swap. Keep in mind too, that Solaris on SPARC simply doesn't support WINE.

Preparation

Many WINE administrators will have to load and configure not only WINE itself but also a version of Intel UNIX, and that version's implementation of X-Window. This section describes doing both, in both the Caldera and the Red Hat environments. Because Sun and SCO systems most frequently are pre-installed and pre-configured, we've omitted coverage of those platforms.

The Caldera environment

Under OpenLinux 2.2, installation is entirely GUI-driven.

 Tip

It's our opinion that, for those whose background is entirely or largely in Windows environments, OpenLinux 2.2 is the best choice for a WINE OS platform, precisely because its installation is so Windows-like.

Installing and configuring OpenLinux 2.2

Caldera's Linux Installation Wizard (*Lizard*) assumes that Windows NT, and no other operating system, is present on the PC to which OpenLinux will be loaded. If this is not the case, you must first install what Caldera refers to as Preparation Components. Once this has been done, you can proceed to completing the installation of OpenLinux 2.2 with Lizard.

Installing preparation components Carrying out these steps will load Caldera's Preparation Components.

1. Place the Installation CD 1 in the drive.

2. If Windows does not automatically run the Caldera Systems OpenLinux Tools utility, launch that program by clicking Start ⇨ Run and then entering the path **D:\winsetup\setup**, where *D:* represents your CD-ROM drive.

3. Choose Install Products from the initial Tools screen.

4. Choose Install Products ⇨ Full Install Preparation.

5. Choose the appropriate language for your implementation from those provided with the Full Install Preparation option.

6. After the resulting Setup progress bar completes, click the Next button in the OpenLinux Install Preparation initial screen.

7. After reviewing Caldera's Software License Agreement and clicking Next, use the resulting dialog to define the directory to which the Windows components of OpenLinux will be installed.

8. Click Next, confirm that the highlighted directory which is then presented is that which you specified, and click Next again.

At this point, you should return to the Install Products menu, and the installation of Caldera's Windows-based tools should be complete.

Creating an installation diskette To verify that you can proceed to creating installation and other diskettes, or to partitioning your drive in preparation for installing OpenLinux, use Windows Explorer to verify that the appropriate OpenLinux tools have been installed

Installation diskettes may be used to launch the installation of OpenLinux. Such diskettes are ordinarily used only if a system cannot boot from its CD-ROM drive. If you need to create such a diskette, follow these instructions.

1. Place a blank, formatted, high-density 3.5-inch diskette in your diskette drive.

2. From Windows, choose Start ⇨ Programs ⇨ OpenLinux ⇨ Create Install Disk.

3. Follow the instructions presented.

Creating module diskettes Caldera's toolkit allows you to create, in addition to installation diskettes, what are called module diskettes. These house hardware drivers which may be needed during the installation of OpenLinux. To create a module diskette, follow these steps:

1. Place a blank, formatted, high-density 3.5 inch diskette in your diskette drive.

2. From Windows, choose Start ⇨ Programs ⇨ OpenLinux ⇨ Create Module Diskette.

3. Follow the instructions presented.

Preparing your hard drive In order to use the tools Caldera provides to partition your hard drive in preparation for installing OpenLinux, you must first install the version of Partition Magic provided with OpenLinux 2.2. Then you can use that application to create a Linux partition.

Installing partition magic To install Partition Magic, follow these steps:

1. From Windows, choose Start ⇨ Programs ⇨ OpenLinux ⇨ Partition and Install Linux.

2. From the resulting dialog, click Next.

3. Confirm or specify the directory to which you wish to install Partition Magic, and then click Next.

4. Confirm or specify the program group to which you wish to install Partition Magic, and then click Next.

From here, you can proceed to using Partition Magic to create an OpenLinux partition.

Creating an OpenLinux partition After installing Partition Magic, your PC should automatically reboot. When it does so, you'll be presented with another Partition Magic dialog, which helps you find free drive space for your OpenLinux partition.

To use this dialog, take these steps.

1. Confirm or specify the Windows partition that Partition Magic has selected as the partition whose size will be reduced in order to provide space for OpenLinux.

2. Specify a size for the OpenLinux partition.

3. Click OK.

Once you've created your Linux partition, you're ready to install OpenLinux 2.2 by means of Lizard.

 Tip

You need not immediately proceed to Lizard. To defer OpenLinux installation, simply reboot to Windows after creating the Linux partition.

Installing with Lizard In order to install OpenLinux 2.2, follow these steps:

1. If you have a bootable **CD-ROM** drive, replace the Caldera CD 1 in that drive, and reboot. If your CD drive is not bootable, place CD 1 in the drive, and put your installation diskette in the diskette drive before rebooting.

2. After rebooting, and as the initial step in installing OpenLinux 2.2, you'll see a screen that reports on the preparation of the OS kernel and the examination of your hardware.

Upon completion of its initial investigations, the Setup utility for OpenLinux asks you to choose the language to be used throughout the installation process. Pick the appropriate language and press Enter.

 Tip

To use the initial Lizard screen effectively, you must: Press the Tab key to move not only among the language selections offered but also among the buttons at the bottom of the screen; use arrow keys to move about within a selected area of the dialog, such as the language list; and press Enter to move to the next screen only when the Next button at the bottom of a dialog is highlighted.

3. To allow the Setup utility to detect and configure your mouse, move the mouse when you've been presented with the appropriate prompt.

4. Scan the drop-down list made available in the resulting dialog. If any of the items provided there, such as ThinkingMouse, pertain to your PC, select that item. Then click Next.

Tip

Once you've configured your mouse, you'll be able to use it throughout the rest of the installation process.

5. From the next screen, confirm or specify Prepared Partition as the area of your hard drive to which OpenLinux should be loaded.

6. In the next dialog, confirm or specify the size of OpenLinux's root partition.

7. In the screen shown next, format your OpenLinux partitions.

8. From the next window, choose the OpenLinux components you wish to install.

9. In the dialog that follows, specify your keyboard model, layout, and language.

10. From the next screen, choose Probe to fine-tune the configuration of your graphics adapter.

11. Once your graphics adapter has been probed and configured, choose from the next screen the make and model of monitor you're using.

12. From the screen that now appears, choose your default video mode and color depth. If you care to, you can also use this dialog to test your display.

13. With the next dialog, define a password for the root user. This individual, also known as the superuser, has virtually unlimited powers on any Unix system.

14. With the next window, define user names and passwords for all other users.

15. From the next screen, define the networking characteristics of OpenLinux.

16. From OpenLinux's final installation dialog, set date and time for OpenLinux.

Upon completing Step 16, you'll have finished installing OpenLinux 2.2.

Installing and configuring X Window

If you successfully complete the Windows and Lizard installation and configuring of OpenLinux 2.2, the components of the X Window system will have been installed and configured automatically. Those components are

- The X server, which provides the protocols that handle the most basic communications between the operating system and your PC's video adapter

- The windows manager, analogous to Microsoft's 32-bit Graphics Driver Interface (GDI), which handles windows and objects within windows

- The Desktop, with its tools, icons, and utilities for GUI-based system management

The Red Hat environment

Under earlier versions of Red Hat Linux such as 5.1, with which we worked in preparing this book, installation relies completely on text menus. Under version 6.0 of Red Hat, the OS's most recent release, installation has become somewhat more GUI-driven. However, even the Red Hat 6.0 installer lacks the features that make the setup of Caldera OpenLinux 2.2 so easy and convenient. Among the missing are

- Preparation components such as partitioning tools and the ability to create installation and module diskettes via a GUI

- The ability to configure mouse and keyboard through dialogs

- The ability to fine-tune graphics performance

- The ability to define, by means of dialogs, file system sizes and mount points

As a result, this section covers only those aspects of Red Hat Linux 6.0 installation we consider most significant. Should you need to load this OS, you can find its complete installation guide at `www.redhat.com/corp/support/manuals/RHL-6.0-Manual/install-guide/manual/doc001.html`.

Hardware support

The Red Hat 6.0 installer can detect not only typical hardware components, but also

- Most Symmetric Multi Processor (SMP)–capable motherboards
- RAID controllers such as AMI MegaRaid, DAC 960, and Compaq SmartArray

Installation methods

Among the features which characterize Red Hat 6.0's installation are

- The need for only one boot disk, with a second such disk required only to support PCMCIA functions during installation
- The ability to install either from an FTP or HTTP server
- The ability to install from a hard drive image

Hardware inventory

Red Hat recommends that, before you begin to install its Linux 6.0, you compile an inventory of your system's characteristics that includes

- The number, size, and type of hard drives, as well as whether those drives are IDE or SCSI, and if the drives are being accessed in LBA mode
- The amount of installed RAM
- Your CD-ROM drive's interface type (IDE, SCSI, or other) and, for non-IDE/non-SCSI drives, the make and model number
- The make and model of SCSI adapters, if any
- The make and model of network cards, if any
- The mouse's type (serial, PS/2, or bus mouse), protocol (Microsoft, Logitech, MouseMan, etc.), and number of buttons
- For serial mice, the port to which the mouse is connected
- The make and model of your video adapter, as well as the chipset it uses, and the amount of video RAM it offers
- The make and model of your monitor, along with its ranges for horizontal and vertical refresh rates

Chapter 2

Installation

Chapter 2 presents particulars on downloading, installing, and configuring WINE.

Downloading

WINE can be downloaded and installed either as precompiled binaries, or as source code that must then be compiled before being configured. We'll discuss both methods in this section.

Tip

When this book went to press, WINE was also available as part of two commercial Linux distributions: SuSE and Caldera.

Pre-compiled binaries

Almost-ready-to-roll WINE executables exist for several Intel UNIX OSes. Here is a list of sites from which some of these binaries may be downloaded. The list includes, where possible, details such as file format.

- For FreeBSD: from `ftp://ftp.freebsd.org/pub/FreeBSD/packages-stable/emulators/`; the file format available is .tgz

- For Red Hat Linux 5.*x*: or Caldera OpenLinux 2.*x* from `http://www.qbc.clic.net/~krynos/`; file formats available are .tar, .gz, and .rpm

- For Solaris x86: from `http://www.ecn.purdue.edu/~laird/WINE/`; the file format available is stripped binary

We have worked with every site just mentioned. Our informal benchmarks of download times for each of these version/site combinations elicited a mean download time of 27 seconds for a T-1 line, and 90 seconds for a 56 Kbps modem.

Source

Downloading WINE's source code is easier, in at least one respect, than obtaining its executables — source can be gotten either by FTP or through the Web. The following is a list of FTP sites that offer WINE's source.

- `ftp://metalab.unc.edu/pub/Linux/ALPHA/wine/` `development/Wine-990328.tar.gz`
- `ftp://tsx-11.mit.edu/pub/linux/ALPHA/Wine/` `development/Wine-990328.tar.gz`
- `ftp://ftp.infomagic.com/pub/mirrors/linux/` `sunsite/ALPHA/wine/development/Wine-990328.tar.gz`
- `ftp://ftp.progsoc.uts.edu.au/pub/Wine/` `development/Wine-990328.tar.gz`

Via the Web, WINE source can be obtained from `http://metalab.unc.edu/pub/Linux/ALPHA/wine/development/`.

Documentation

Documentation available online from the WINE Project comes in many forms, including

- Overview of the suite
- FAQ
- Man pages
- Programmer's reference manual
- Source documentation

The code fragment below, drawn from a sample makefile, gives you an idea of what's included in the last of these documentation categories. We'll examine a few lines from this sample more closely in Table 2-1, which follows it.

Tip

Those of you unfamiliar with compiling C or other source code under Unix may not recognize the term makefile. A makefile is simply a batch file that sets the conditions under which the compilation will take place, and the characteristics it will assign to the executable it produces.

```
SHELL    = /bin/sh
CC    = gcc
CPP      = gcc -E
CFLAGS   = -g -O2 -Wall
OPTIONS  = -D_REENTRANT
X_CFLAGS = -I/usr/X11R6/include
X_LIBS   = -L/usr/X11R6/lib
```

Table 2-1 *Examining some of a WINE Makefile's Contents*

This Line	Accomplishes This
SHELL=/bin/sh	Assigns the symbolic name SHELL to the shell
CC = gcc	Assigns the alias CC to the GNU C compiler as WINE's compiler of choice
CPP = gcc -E	Assigns the alias CPP to the GNU C preprocessor, used with the -E option, telling WINE to run *only* the preprocessor, rather than carrying out a full compilation
OPTIONS = -D_REENTRANT	States that WINE will be compiled so as to be able to use multi-threading-safe versions of the operating system's include files
X_CFLAGS = -I/usr/X11R6/include	tells WINE which directory to search for X-Windows related files to be included at compile time as a result of the preprocessor directive `#include`
X_LIBS = -L/usr/X11R6/lib	Tells WINE which directory to search for X Window-related files to be linked into the executable at compile time

We found the man pages and the programmer's reference to be the most helpful. But Table 2-2 describes what we feel to be the relative strengths and shortcomings of all of these documents.

Table 2-2 *Documenting WINE*

This Form	Offers	But Lacks
overview of the suite	An excellent introduction to WINE	Definitions of some terms, such as GDI (*Graphics Driver Interface*, a Windows display driver).
FAQ	A few specific clues to installing and configuring WINE	Effective organization, presenting categories of information seemingly at random.
man pages	The best overall discussion of what's needed to obtain, install, configure, and run WINE	Definitions of some terms such as feature and DLL names.
programmer's reference manual	In-depth discussions of significant WINE design features	Completeness; at the time this book was being written, major sections were incomplete or missing entirely.
source documentation	Some detail on important issues such as debugging and working with fonts and printers	Any indication of the importance to WINE of the topics covered. For example, the item *programs* simply links to a request for further information on creating tests for WINE.

Tip

In addition to these WINE docs, we'd suggest that those of you without a strong background in C, object-oriented, and/or X Window programming keep references relating to these topics on hand when compiling and configuring WINE.

Installing

Getting WINE onto a system takes little time or effort; much of the process has been at least partially automated. We'll begin by examining the type of installation for which this is particularly true: loading precompiled WINE binaries. Then we'll move on to discussing the more involved means of installing WINE — compiling its source.

Using Pre-compiled binaries

Installing WINE from preexisting binaries is a snap. Just follow these steps.

1. Once you've downloaded, unzip with the command appropriate to the format you pulled down.

   - For .tar files (files archived with the tar command), use `tar xvf` <*name of file you just downloaded*>

   - For .gz files (files compressed with the GNU zip, or gzip, utility), use `gunzip` <*name of file you just downloaded*>

   - For .rpm files (files created with the Red Hat Linux Package Management utility), use `rpm -i` <*name of file you just downloaded*>

2. Ensure that the WINE executable, called simply wine, and its companion executable dosmod, the DOS program loader, reside in the path /usr/local/bin, if you've installed WINE yourself, or in the possible alternate path /usr/X11R6/ if you happen to have a preinstalled version of WINE. If necessary, use the cp or mv command to place these files.

3. Ensure that WINE's global configuration file, wine.conf, resides in the path /usr/local/etc. If necessary, use the cp or mv command to make sure that they do.

4. Ensure that WINE's global symbol table, wine.sym, resides in the path /usr/local/lib. If necessary, use the cp or mv command to place the symbol table.

Using source

While it presents you with more complexity, installing WINE from source code also offers advantages, first among them the ability to customize, to some degree at least, your WINE implementation as you compile it. That ability rests primarily on a single category of information supplied at compile time: configuration options.

Options

A total of 32 options may be supplied to WINE at compile time, and these will significantly affect WINE's operating characteristics. The following sections outline what we consider to be the most important of these options.

cache-file

Syntax: ./configure *-cache-file* = *FILE*, where *FILE* represents the path name of the file to which you wish to cache the results of the tests of the execution of the configure run.

help

Syntax: ./configure *-help*, to produce a list of WINE's configuration options.

no-create

Syntax: ./configure *-no-create*, to run the configuration tests without producing output files.

quiet, or silent

Syntax: ./configure *-quiet, or ./configure -silent*, to compile WINE while forgoing its standard *checking* ... messages.

bindir

Syntax: ./configure *-bindir* = *DIR*, where *DIR* represents the path name of the directory in which WINE's user executables will be found.

datadir

Syntax: ./configure *-datadir* = *DIR*, where *DIR* represents the path name of the directory in which WINE's read-only, architecture-independent data will be found.

sysconfdir

Syntax: `./configure` *-sysconfdir DIR,* where *DIR* represents the path name of the directory in which WINE's read-only, machine-specific data will be found.

libdir

Syntax: `./configure` *-libdir* = *DIR,* where *DIR* represents the path name of the directory in which WINE's object code libraries will be found.

includedir

Syntax: `./configure` *-includedir* = *DIR,* where *DIR* represents the path name of the directory in which WINE's C header files will be found.

mandir

Syntax: `./configure` *-mandir* = *DIR,* where *DIR* represents the path name of the directory in which WINE's man documentation will be found.

x-inxludes

Syntax: `./configure` *-x-includes* = *DIR,* where *DIR* represents the path name of the directory in which the include files pertaining to X that WINE will use can be found.

x-libraries

Syntax: `./configure` *-x-libraries* = *DIR,* where *DIR* represents the path name of the directory in which the X libraries WINE will use can be found.

The configure utility At compile time, supply configuration options to WINE-in-the-making through the utility configure. Assuming you're working in the top level source directory, the syntax for this command would be

```
./configure -option_name
```

After configure runs, two more steps must also be taken, in this order:

```
make depend; make
make install
```

The first of these make commands creates the WINE executable; the second installs it.

Configuring

By far the most important of WINE's configuration files are its global file /usr/local/etc/wine.conf, and possible user-specific configuration files, .winerc.

The global configuration file

Whether your WINE configuration begins with binaries or source, it will rely heavily on WINE's global configuration file. WINE expects to have its runtime characteristics defined in the file /usr/local/etc/wine.conf. But you may also sketch out WINE's personality with

- The file .winerc, in a user's home directory
- A file of any name in any directory, as long as that file is pointed to by the operating system environment variable WINE_INI
- WINE's -sysconfdir option to configure, supplied directly from the command line

If you use a file to describe WINE's traits, that file must follow certain rules.

Configuration file sections

Wherever it lives, a WINE configuration file must group entries in sections. Each such section must be identified with a line of the form

```
[section name]
```

What's more, a WINE configuration file should contain a unique section for every device associated with its platform. So, if your system includes

- a hard drive with a DOS and a Linux partition
- A diskette drive
- A CD-ROM drive
- A serial port
- A parallel port

your WINE configuration file must include a section for each of these devices. Each such section will control the behavior of the device under WINE.

For the PC on which this book was written, two of WINE's hardware-related configuration file sections looked like this.

```
[Drive C]
Path=/mnt/win95
Type=hd
Label=DOS-C
Filesystem=msdos
Device=/dev/hda1
[Drive D]
Path=/mnt/cdrom
Type=cdrom
Label=CDROM
Filesystem=win95
```

Another section that should be included in any WINE configuration file is one that dictates WINE's appearance. Most often, this section causes WINE to look as much as possible like Windows 9x, but you can give it other demeanors. Once again, here's a look at how this aspect of WINE was defined on the PC on which this book was written.

```
[Tweak.Layout]
WineLook=Win95
```

Within configuration file sections

Inside any section of a WINE configuration file, individual lines other than the section identifier must be of the form

```
parameter=value
```

Lines of this pattern must pertain to the section name which most immediately precedes them.

Value can be any text string. You needn't enclose value in quotes, but if you choose to do so, for readability or any other reason, either single or double quotation marks will suffice.

Configuration file specifications

This section spells out the WINE Project's requirements for a configuration file.

[Drive X]

Since most Windows applications expect a DOS- or Windows-like drive and directory scheme, you must include one such section for every drive with which you want WINE to be able to work.

Path = rootdirectory

This first parameter in a Drive section should indicate the portion of the PC Unix file system under which you mounted your Microsoft partition. For instance, your version of this line might read

```
Path=/win95
```

Type = type

With this line in **wine.conf**, you can specify the type of drive you're defining. WINE supports the following drive types:

- Diskette drives: floppy
- Hard drives: hd
- CD-ROM drives: cdrom
- Network drives: network

Label = label

You can specify a drive — that is, a volume — label with this configuration file entry. However, the label argument must be no more than 11 characters.

Serial = serial

This Drive section entry can specify the serial number of the device in question. Only eight-character hexadecimal numbers may be supplied for the serial argument.

Filesystem = fstype

This configuration file entry, used to specify the type of file system WINE should emulate, and whose default fstype value is win95, can use any of the values:

- msdos (FAT16)
- win95 (vfat)
- unix

Tip

The WINE Project recommends using win95 to emulate any of ext2fs, VFAT and FAT32, and specifying msdos only if you *must* simulate a FAT16 file system. Further, the project urges no use of the value unix for the fstype argument unless you intend to port applications to WINE by using its library WINELIB; avoiding FAT16; and relying primarily on the win95 fstype.

[wine]

This section header signals the definition of various Windows-related paths to WINE.

windows = directory

You can use an entry of this sort to tell WINE to look for Windows files in a path other than the default of C:\WINDOWS.

system = directory

If you need to specify a Windows System directory other than the default C\WINDOWS\SYSTEM, supply the path appropriate to your environment in the directory argument.

temp = directory

To tell WINE the directory where Windows applications can store temporary files, supply an appropriate value for the directory argument, in DOS notation, such as *C:\WINDOWS\TEMP*.

path = <directory names separated by semicolons>

As its default value of C:\WINDOWS;C:\WINDOWS\SYSTEM indicates, the directory names argument sets out the path where WINE will look for executable and .DLL files.

symboltablefile = filename

You must tell WINE the path and file name of the symbol table to be used by its built-in debugger by supplying a correct value for the filename argument.

[DllDefaults]

This section header alerts WINE to information regarding any additional libraries it may require.

EXTRA_LD_LIBRARY_PATH = /usr/local/lib/wine:[/more/paths/to/search]

The configuration parameter EXTRA_LD_LIBRARY_PATH, with its accompanying arguments, specifies any additional paths to be searched by WINE for certain DLL and other libraries.

DefaultLoadOrder = native,elfdll,so,builtin

The comma-separated list of module types which serves as the argument to the DefaultLoadOrder parameter specifies the order in which WINE will try to load DLLs into memory. If DefaultLoadOrder is not defined, WINE will load DLLs in this sequence:

1. native
2. elfdll
3. so
4. builtin

[DllOverrides]

This section header, and its following comma-separated list of DLLs, can be used to define the load order for any modules it discusses.

kernel32, gdi32, user32 = builtin

Such an entry in the DllOverrides section would ensure that the three core components of Windows 95, that is

- kernel32, the 32-bit OS kernel
- gdi32, the 32-bit Graphics Driver Interface
- user32, the 32-bit user interface to Windows

would all be loaded as built-in DLLs.

Tip

The WINE Project advises us *not* to specify loading the kernel, kernel32, gdi, gdi32, user, or user32 modules as anything other than built -in DLLs. Failing to observe this caution may cause WINE to fail, since the suite cannot work with native Windows versions of these libraries. Nor do the members of the Project anticipate that WINE in its native version will ever be able to use kernel32. As a result, there is usually no need to change the DLLOverrides section.

[DllPairs]

This section header, as the WINE Project describes it, is intended to identify DLLs that cannot live without each other unless they are loaded in the same format.

Tip

The Project team points out further that defining such pairings does not guarantee either that the pairs in question will in fact be loaded as the same type of DLL or that correct versions of either member of the pair will be loaded. The team suggests, as a result, that this section too be left unaltered. Note also that this section header and any values included under it may not be present in future versions of WINE.

[serialports]

The serialports section header begins the definition of WINE's handling of these communications ports.

com[12345678] = devicename

Entries that begin with the specification of a COM port in the DOS fashion, such as *COM1*, associate a Linux device designation with that port in order to define the devices which WINE will recognize as any of COM1 through COM8 inclusive. For example, the typical device designation for COM1 is */dev/ttyS0*.

[parallelports]

The parallelports section header begins the definition of WINE's handling of printer devices and ports.

lpt[12345678] = devicename

Entries which begin with the specification of an lpt port in Microsoft style, such as lpt1, associate a Linux device designation with that port in order to define print devices to WINE.

[spy]

This section header indicates the beginning of definitions relating to WINE's logging.

file = filename

This entry tells WINE, with the filename argument, where the suite should place its log file. Note that supplying the value CON for the filename argument causes WINE to log to standard output — that is, to the console.

exclude = <message names separated by semicolons>

This entry can be used to specify which messages you wish excluded from WINE's log file.

include = <message names separated by semicolons>

This entry can define messages you want to ensure are included in WINE's log file.

[Tweak.Layout]

This section header indicates definitions of WINE's look or overall resemblance to a specific Windows version.

WINELook = *<Windows Version>*

If you wish applications running under WINE to appear as they would when running under Windows 9*x*, supply the value Win95 for the Windows Version argument. Other possible values, and the appearances that will result from them, are

- win31: for a Windows 3.*x* appearance
- win98: for a Windows 98 appearance

Remember, the WINELook parameter affects only *the appearance* of WINE, not its behavior. Both 16- and 32-bit applications run as they otherwise would, even when this option is changed.

An example of wine.conf

The following sections constitute the complete text of our own wine.conf. Each section header represents a single line in that file and is accompanied by a brief explanation of the line in question.

[Drive A]

Its enclosing square brackets tell WINE that this line marks the beginning of a section in wine.conf. The phrase Drive A tells WINE further that it's going to learn about its host PC's floppy drive in this section.

Path = /mnt/floppy

This line specifies the point in the Linux file system which has been associated with WINE's floppy drive, that is, the path /mnt/floppy.

Type = floppy

Type=floppy leaves nothing to WINE's imagination, telling the suite that the device in question, whatever its DOS drive letter, is indeed a floppy drive.

Label = Floppy

In order to allow WINE to apply, if necessary, an appropriate volume label to the device being defined, we included this optional line in wine.conf.

Filesystem = win95

After reading this line, WINE knows that files on the floppy will be handled as Windows 95 files, that is, as FAT 32.

Serial =

As you may have already guessed, the Serial = ... line is another optional item in **wine.conf**. Failing to supply a serial-number argument will have no impact on WINE's performance. Nor will omitting this line entirely do WINE any harm.

Device = /dev/fd0

With Path=/mnt/floppy, WINE learned of its floppy drive's place in the Linux file system. With Device=/dev/fd0, the suite discovers that the device in question may be accessed at what's called low level — that is, the device may be formatted.

[Drive C]

With enclosing square brackets and the phrase Drive C, WINE knows that it's going to learn in this section about its host PC's first hard drive.

Path = /mnt/win95

This line specifies the point in the Linux file system that has been associated with WINE's primary hard drive.

Type = hd

Once again ensuring that WINE won't misunderstand, this line informs the suite that the drive being defined is indeed a hard drive.

Label = DOS-C

We gave WINE a suitable volume label for its hard drive by placing this optional line in wine.conf.

Filesystem = msdos

WINE now knows that files on Drive C should be handled as MS-DOS files — that is, as FAT 16.

Device = /dev/hda1

With this line, WINE discovers its hard drive's device designation under Linux.

[Drive D]

Reading this line tells WINE it's about to encounter another wine.conf section which deals with a storage device.

Path = /mnt/cdrom

Here, WINE learns that the path under Linux to the device in question is /mnt/cdrom.

Type = cdrom

This line tells WINE that both Drive D and /mnt/cdrom indicate a CD-ROM device.

Label = CDROM

Optional like its earlier analogs, this line gives WINE an appropriate volume label to associate with our CD drive.

Filesystem = win95

After reading this line, WINE knows that files on any CDs should be dealt with as Windows 95 files.

[wine]

This section header literally tells WINE about its own characteristics and behavior.

Windows = c:\windows

Here, WINE receives the MS-DOS path to whatever Microsoft operating system it must work with.

System = c:\windows\system

This line tells WINE the location within the DOS file system of the Windows System directory.

Temp = c:\windows\temp

This line gives WINE the location within the DOS file system of the directory Windows uses to house temporary work files, that is, of the Windows Temp directory.

Path = c:\windows;c:\windows\system; c:\msoffice\winword;c:\msoffice\excel

We used this line to tell WINE the portions of the DOS file system it should search for applications it's asked to run.

SymbolTableFile = /usr/local/lib/wine.sym

This entry in wine.conf supplies the full path name within the Linux file system of WINE's symbol table—that is, its complete listing of all symbolic names used in its source code.

printer = on

With this line, WINE learns that applications it manages will have access to a printer.

[options]

This section header tells WINE it's about to learn more about those aspects of its behavior that can vary.

AllocSystemColors = 100

AllocSystemColors = 100 tells WINE that it will have a palette made up of a total of 100 colors.

[fonts]

This section header informs WINE that its font capabilities are about to be defined.

Resolution = 96

By supplying the value 96, we took the WINE Project's advice and specified that our WINE implementation would work with a mid-sized font. Values used with this configuration parameter should be in the range 60–120, with larger fonts resulting from larger values.

Default = -adobe-times-

Because of this entry, WINE will use Adobe-Times as its default font. Adobe-Times maps to or is functionally analogous to the widely used Windows font Times New Roman.

[serialports]

The serialports section header tells WINE to expect details relating to the serial ports with which it will work.

COM1 = /dev/ttyS0

This line specifies the Linux device designation associated with WINE's first serial port.

COM2 = /dev/ttyS1

This line gives WINE the Linux device designation for its second serial port.

COM3 = /dev/ttyS2

Here WINE learns the Linux device designation for its third serial port.

COM4 = /dev/ttyS3

Finally, WINE discovers the Linux device designation for its fourth serial port.

[parallelports]

This section header tells WINE that information regarding the parallel ports with which it will work is forthcoming.

Lpt1 = /dev/lp1

With this line, WINE learns the Linux device designation for its single parallel port.

[spooler]

The spooler section header tells WINE that the definitions that follow relate to its handling of spooling operations — that is, of directing jobs to a printer.

LPT1: = |lpr

After reading this line, WINE knows that any jobs directed by Windows applications to something called LPT1 should in fact be piped to the Linux lpr command.

LPT2: = |lpr

This line tells WINE that any jobs directed to LPT should be piped to the Linux lpr command.

LPT3: = /dev/lp3

Rather than instructing WINE to pipe output, this wine.conf entry tells it to redirect jobs intended for LPT3 to the Linux device /dev/lp3.

[spy]

With this section header, we alerted WINE to details to follow regarding its logging activities.

Exclude = WM_SIZE;WM_TIMER;

This entry tells WINE to forgo messages regarding the size of and timer used by its window manager.

[Tweak.Layout]

This section header lets WINE know that the appearance or look of its applications' display is about to be defined.

WINELook = Win95

The final entry in our wine.conf instructs WINE to make applications' displays resemble those they would have under Windows 95.

The Effect of OS Environment Variables

Be aware that WINE uses the existing environment of the shell from which it is started to run the Windows or DOS programs it presents. Therefore, these environment variables can have a significant impact on how those programs perform. We'll use the following sections to elaborate on what we feel to be the most important of these environmental parameters.

DISPLAY

This environment variable, controlling as it does the placement of screen displays under X Windows, can obviously affect the presentation of applications under WINE. Setting this variable to its typical 0:0 value will help ensure smooth displays of WINE-driven applications. Note also that this or any other manipulation of the DISPLAY environment variable can be done from the command line, when WINE is launched, by means of the -display option discussed later in this chapter.

PATH

Clearly, should a user's environment not include a definition of the path where WINE can be found, that user will be able to run WINE only with difficulty.

User-specific configuration files

One might expect that user-specific configuration files would ordinarily be less extensive than wine.conf, and would contain only settings intended to overrride those found in the global configuration file. Unfortunately, at the time this book was being written, this was not the case. The file .winerc needs to be a copy of WINE's global configuration file.

Configuring at the Command Line

As was the case with compilation, WINE's configuration can be customized from the command line.

Options

Nearly two dozen options may be supplied to WINE from the command line as the suite is being launched. These options can significantly affect WINE's operating characteristics. The following sections outline what we consider to be the most important of these options.

backingstore

Context: Window Management

Syntax: ./wine -*backingstore*

The backingstore option, when used at the WINE command line, allows the suite to remember areas of windows that have become obscured by other windows. When backingstore is enabled, therefore, WINE need not completely redraw such backgrounded windows, should they be brought back to the foreground. Note that enabling backingstore causes the X server to demand more memory but speeds up the presentation of application windows.

config filename

Context: Configuration File

Syntax: ./wine -*config newfilename*

Supplying the config option with an accompanying, appropriate file name such as the example given above causes WINE to substitute the named file for either of WINE's default configuration files. This option can therefore be used to customize WINE's implementation.

debug

Context: Debugging

Syntax: ./wine -*debug*

Supplying the debug option at the command line starts the WINE debugger before starting WINE, thereby improving your ability to debug applications' performance under WINE.

debugmsg

Context: Debugging

Syntax: ./wine -debugmsg <feature names and other parameters>

The debugmsg option turns on or off debugging messages which are specific to many aspects of WINE. Using the debugmsg option when launching WINE allows you to focus on what might be causing problems with the suite.

depth n

Context: Memory Use, Screen Display

Syntax: ./wine -depth 3

Specifying the depth option and an accompanying, appropriate integer value means specifying the depth multi-window screens can reach under WINE — that is, the number of windows that can be stacked on WINE's display.

desktop geom

Context: Screen Display

Syntax: ./wine -desktop integer x integer

The desktop option helps to define the shape of WINE's display. Specifically, this option allows the user to encase WINE's displayed output within a window of the specified x and y coordinates. So, for example, the command

```
./wine -desktop 640x480
```

would cause the output of any applications running under WINE to be enclosed in a window of the indicated dimensions.

display name

Context: Screen Display

Syntax: ./wine -display hostname:0

The display option specifies the X11 server which will respond to WINE's display requests. The parameter :0 enforces use of the local X display, while a parameter of the form hostname:0 would attempt to use the X server of the host indicated by hostname. Note that in order for the latter syntax to succeed, the requesting station and user must be authorized to use the indicated remote X server.

dll name

Context: Library Management

Syntax: ./wine *-dll commdlg=n*

The dll option and its accompanying arguments detail the override type and load order to be used when including WINE DLLs in its runtime. At the time this book was being prepared, four types of libraries could be loaded into a process's address space:

- built-in
- external
- native
- special

Every DLL named with this option may have its own unique load order. If you specify a load order, you specify which version of the DLL in question WINE will try to load first, and then, if that initial load fails, which version it will attempt to load next, and so on. Multiple libraries that require the same load order can be indicated as a single, comma-separated argument list.

For example, the partial command line

```
-dll comdlg32,commdlg=n,b
```

tells WINE to try to load the DLLs comdlg32 and commdlg first as native Windows libraries, and, should that effort fail, to try then to include their built-in versions.

Tip

The WINE Project recommends ensuring that DLL pairs, such as comdlg32 and commdlg, have exactly the same load order, so as to preclude runtime errors which might result from mismatches between the versions of related libraries.

Fortunately, the DLL names which you may indicate to WINE number fewer than half as many as its debugging channel names. The following sections detail these DLLs.

advapi32

Context: Advanced APIs, such as those controlling security and encryption

Syntax: ./wine *-dll advapi32=*

avifile

Context: Multimedia

Syntax: ./wine *-dll avifile=*

> **Tip**
>
> The WINE Project recommends using the native version of avifile, the Audio Video Interleave, an audio/video standard developed by Microsoft but not yet fully implemented in WINE.

comctl32

Context: Display Controls

Syntax: ./wine *-dll comctl32=*

Configuring the comctl32 DLL into WINE results in the runtime's having access to 32-bit common controls.

comdlg32

Context: Dialogs

Syntax: ./wine *-dll comdlg32=*

Providing WINE the comdlg32 DLL supplies it with the 32-bit Common Dialog Library.

compobj

Context: Object Linking and Embedding

Syntax: ./wine *-dll compobj=*

Supplying the compobj DLL to WINE gives the suite access to a 16- and 32-bit OLE interoperability library.

crtdll

Context: Windows 9x Applications

Syntax: ./wine *-dll crtdll=*

Including crtdll in WINE's command-line mix makes the Microsoft C runtime library available to applications running under the suite.

dciman32

Context: Screen Display

Syntax: ./wine *-dll dciman32=*

Providing the dciman32 DLL to WINE also provides it a display control interface library.

ddeml

Context: Interprocess Communication

Syntax: ./wine *-dll ddeml=*

Incorporating the ddeml DLL into WINE gives the suite a set of Direct Data Exchange (*DDE*) messaging libraries. DDE, or, as Microsoft originally called it, Dynamic Data Linking (*DDL*), is a Windows 3.*x* protocol that allows application programs to communicate using a client-server model. When a server — or, in DDE parlance, a *publisher* — modifies part of a document shared by applications, clients or subscribers automatically learn of the changes and incorporate them in their own copy of the item.

gdi32

Context: Screen Display

Syntax: ./wine *-dll gdi32=*

How, and how well, WINE works with 32-bit Graphical Driver Interfaces can be affected by supplying the GDI32 name with the dll option when launching WINE.

Tip

The WINE Project recommends using the WINE implementation of the GDI32 DLL. Supplying the =n parameter to this option/name combination at the command line can create rather than resolve problems; at the time this book was being written, the native version of GDI32 and WINE could not work together.

keyboard

Context: Keyboard Input

Syntax: ./wine *-dll keyboard=*

Facilitate WINE's managing of keyboard behavior and characteristics by controlling the loading of this DLL.

lz32

Context: Compression and Decompression

Syntax: ./wine *-dll lz32=*

Help WINE handle the compression and decompression of data on drives by controlling the loading of this DLL.

lzexpand

Context: Compression and Decompression

Syntax: ./wine *-dll lzexpand=*

mmsystem

Context: Multimedia

Syntax: ./wine *-dll mmsystem=*

Incorporate multimedia functionality into WINE by controlling how the core multimedia DLL mmsystem is loaded.

mouse

Context: Mouse Input

Syntax: ./wine *-dll mouse=*

Maximize WINE's ability to interpret and manage mouse behavior and characteristics by controlling how this DLL is loaded.

mpr

Context: Networking

Syntax: ./wine -*dll mpr=*

Help WINE to offer full network functionality by controlling the loading of this 32-bit Windows network interface DLL.

msnet32

Context: Networking

Syntax: ./wine -*dll msnet32*

Control the loading of this DLL in order to give WINE access to the API library for 32-bit Microsoft networking.

msvfw32

Context: Multimedia

Syntax: ./wine -*dll vfw32=*

Help to give WINE access to a 32-bit runtime library for Microsoft's handling of video by controlling the loading of the msvfw32 DLL.

ole2

Context: Object Linking and Embedding

Syntax: ./wine -*dll ole2=*

Control the loading of this DLL in order to facilitate WINE's work with version 2 OLE objects.

ole2conv

Context: Object Linking and Embedding

Syntax: ./wine -*dll ole2conv=*

Improve WINE's ability to use the QuickDraw graphic import filter by controlling the loading of the OLE2CONV DLL.

ole2disp

Context: Object Linking and Embedding

Syntax: ./wine *-dll ole2disp=*

Improve WINE's access to the OLE 2.1 16- and 32-bit interoperability library by controlling the loading of this DLL.

ole2nls

Context: Object Linking and Embedding

Syntax: ./wine *-dll ole2nls=*

Improve WINE's access to the OLE 2.1 16- and 32-bit interoperability library by controlling the loading of the OLE2NLS DLL.

ole32

Context: Object Linking and Embedding

Syntax: ./wine *-dll ole32=*

Controlling the loading of the OLE32 DLL may help WINE properly handle 32-bit OLE 2.0 components.

oleaut32

Context: Object Linking and Embedding

Syntax: ./wine *-dll oleaut32=*

Controlling the loading of this DLL can affect WINE's ability to work properly with 32-bit OLE automation.

olecli

Context: Object Linking and Embedding

Syntax: ./wine *-dll olecli=*

Improve WINE's access to the 16-bit client library for Object Linking and Embedding by controlling the loading of the OLECLI DLL.

olecli32

Context: Object Linking and Embedding

Syntax: ./wine *-dll olecli32=*

Improve WINE's access to the 32-bit client library for Object Linking and Embedding by controlling the loading of the OLECLI DLL.

olecnv32

Context: Object Linking and Embedding

Syntax: ./wine *-dll olecnv32=*

Control the loading of the OLECNV32 DLL in order to improve WINE's access to the 32-bit OLE 2.0 components.

oledlg

Context: Object Linking and Embedding

Syntax: ./wine *-dll oledlg=*

Affect WINE's ability to support Microsoft's OLE 2.0 user interface by controlling the loading of this DLL.

olesvr

Context: Object Linking and Embedding

Syntax: ./wine *-dll olesvr=*

Affect WINE's access to the server library for OLEby controlling the loading of the OLESVR DLL.

olesvr32

Context: Object Linking and Embedding

Syntax: ./wine *-dll olesvr32=*

Affect WINE's access to the 32-bit Windows OLE server core components by controlling the loading of the OLESVR32 DLL.

olethk32

Context: Object Linking and Embedding

Syntax: ./wine *-dll olethk32=*

Provide WINE with the means to load and jump to the correct OLE-related overlays by controlling the loading of this DLL.

rasapi16

Context: Remote Access

Syntax: ./wine *-dll rasapi16=*

Provide 16-bit client computers with the ability to use Microsoft's Remote Access Service (*RAS*) by providing that service's API with this DLL name.

rasapi32

Context: Remote Access

Syntax: ./wine *-rasapi32=*

Provide 32-bit clients access to *RAS* by controlling the loading of this DLL.

shell

Context: Setup

Syntax: ./wine *-dll shell=*

Control whether you allow applications running under WINE to use the standard Windows 3.1 shell by managing the loading of the SHELL DLL.

win32s16

Context: Application Management

Syntax: ./wine *-dll win32s16=*

You may need to control the loading of this DLL in order to give WINE a means of ensuring application compatibility.

win87em

Context: Emulation

Syntax: ./wine -*dll win87em=*

Ensure that WINE-driven applications can successfully emulate the math libraries of the 80387 processor by controlling the loading of this DLL.

winaspi

Context: SCSI Devices

Syntax: ./wine -*dll winaspi=*

Help ensure WINE's ability to work with devices controlled by software modeled on the *ASPI* SCSI standard by controlling the loading of this DLL.

winmm

Context: Multimedia

Syntax: ./wine -*dll winmm=*

Give WINE the ability to access the core Win32 multimedia library by controlling the loading of this DLL.

winsock

Context: Networking

Syntax: ./wine -*dll winsock=*

Microsoft created the Winsock (Windows Socket) network software specification to describe how applications running under its OSes from Windows 3.*x* to the present can access network services, particularly the TCP/IP protocol suite. Winsock allows any application written to it to work with a protocol implementation from any vendor, provided that implementation is itself Winsock-compatible. Therefore, controlling the loading of this DLL may help ensure proper performance by networking applications running under WINE.

winspool

Context: Printing

Syntax: ./wine *-dll winspool=*

You may be able to improve WINE's interaction with Windows applications' use of spooling, that is, of queueing files for later processing of some kind, by controlling the loading of the WINSPOOL DLL.

Tip

When used without further qualification, the term spool refers to the print spool, or the queue of jobs awaiting delivery to a printer. However, on some occasions, both the generic term and the Windows-specific cognate Winspool have been used to refer to devices such as plotters.

wnaspi32

Context: SCSI Devices

Syntax: ./wine *-dll wnaspi32=*

Help WINE's ability to work with ASPI SCSI devices through a 32-bit API by controlling the loading of this DLL.

wsock32

Context: Networking

Syntax: ./wine *-dll wsock32=*

Controlling the loading of this DLL into WINE's runtime helps ensure proper performance by networking applications running under WINE, by providing them the appropriate 32-bit Windows Sockets API.

failreadonly

Context: File Management

Syntax: ./wine *-failreadonly*

Supplying this option at run time defines how WINE will handle read-only files, denying applications running under WINE the capacity to open read-only files with the ability to write to or modify such files. In particular, applications sometimes try to open read-only files stored on CD-ROM drives as read/write. Ordinarily, WINE would issue a warning when it detected such attempts. However, only by supplying the -failreadonly option from the command line can you cause the suite to consider such efforts as errors.

fixedmap

Context: Screen Display

Syntax: ./wine *-fixedmap*

Including the fixedmap option specifies that WINE will use a small, fixed colormap, thereby providing only a limited number of colors to displays.

iconic

Context: Screen Display

Syntax: ./wine *-iconic*

Starting WINE with the iconic option ensures that WINE will be iconified — that is, will be represented on the display as an icon.

language *name*

Context: Screen Display

Syntax: ./wine *-language Cr*

The language option defines the language to which WINE's text messages and captions, such as those related to buttons, dialogs, and so on, will default. Should you fail to specify a language from the command line with this option, WINE will try to autodetect the appropriate language by examining the operating system environment variable LANG. Possible values for name are

Cr: Croatian	Fi: Finnish	No: Norwegian
Da: Danish	Fr: French	Pl: Polish
De: German	Hu: Hungarian	Po: Portuguese
En: English	It: Italian	Sw: Swedish
Es: Spanish	Ko: Korean	

At the time this book was being written, the WINE Project was in the process of incorporating other languages into WINE's repertoire. These include

Bulgarian	Icelandic	Slovanian
Chinese	Japanese	Turkish
Croatian	Romanian	
Greek	Slovak	

 Tip

While the WINE Project's online documentation lists a possible value of Ca for the configuration option language, this value, at the time this book was being written, was not used.

managed

Context: Memory Management; Screen Display

Syntax: ./wine *-managed*

The managed option directs WINE to handle top-level windows as properly managed X windows. In other words, using this option helps to ensure that applications running under WINE will look like *ordinary* Linux applications.

mode name

Context: Screen Display

Syntax: ./wine *-enhanced* **or** ./wine *--standard*

This option changes the flags WINE reports to a Windows 3.1 application. Specifically, the enhanced option generates a flag which allows WINE to distinguish and switch between standard or 286 mode and enhanced or 386 and higher mode.

application name

Context: Application Management

Syntax: ./wine *-application winword* **or** ./wine *-application /mnt/win95/ msoffice/winword*

The application option and its name parameter define an application which will be launched automatically when WINE starts. Note that it may be necessary to supply the full path name of the application to be launched.

privatemap

Context: Screen Display

Syntax: ./wine -*privatemap*

Running WINE with this option tells the suite to use a private colormap. The effect of such a map is to cause colors to differ between windows running under WINE and any other, purely X, windows. In short, the privatemap option allows WINE-related windows to have their own color scheme.

synchronous

Context: Screen Display

Syntax: ./wine -*synchronous*

The synchronous option launches WINE with synchronous display behavior. But be very cautious in using this option. It is best applied to debugging the behavior of WINE's graphics, and can actually slow down displays. Therefore, synchronous isn't for the *average user*.

winver *number*

Context: Screen Display

Syntax: ./wine -*winver win95*

The winver option and its accompanying argument specify which Windows version WINE should mimic. Possible values for number are

- win31: Windows 3.1
- win95: Windows 95
- nt351: Windows NT 3.51
- nt40: Windows NT 4.0

Be aware as well that WINE does its best to autodetect the version of Windows a given application expects, and will mimic this autodetected version if no other version is specified at the command line.

Tip

Note that, while they are not supported explicitly by means of separate parameters to the winver option, most applications which ordinarily run under Windows 98 or Windows 2000 will perform properly if the win95 parameter is given to winver. That's because this option simply changes the OS version number reported to applications.

Debugging channels

Names in this category can be supplied to WINE from the command line as it's being launched, in order to focus on debugging specific aspects of the behavior of applications running under WINE. Names for debugging channels refer to such diverse WINE characteristics as

- The appearance of display elements like cursor, status bar, tool bar, and tree view
- How the suite handles system-level components such as heaps and sockets

Over 200 debugging channel names exist for WINE. The following sections briefly define what we feel to be a representative sample of those most likely to be helpful in debugging or enhancing the behavior of applications running under WINE.

debugmsg and debugging channel name syntax

To receive debugging information on aspects of WINE, you must supply the name of the appropriate debugging channel, along with the command-line option debugmsg, according to this general syntax.

```
./wine -debugmsg +dll, +x11drv
```

This command will cause the debugger to return all messages relating to DLLs or the X-Windows driver.

Using the debugmsg option in a more sophisticated way requires more involved syntax. A complete example would read as follows.

```
debugmsg [type]#name[,[type]#name][#relay=API]
```

In such usage

- **type** is optional, and can be any of the following: err, indicating error conditions; warn, indicating warnings; fixme, indicating portions of the source code that remain to be optimized; or trace, indicating the desire to do no more than trace the results of incorporating the named feature. If type is not specified, all debugging messages will be turned on.
- **#** is required and can be either + or -.
- No space should occur after the comma between names.
- API represents either the name of an entire Dynamic Linked Library or a single API.
- Relay represents an API.

Table 2-3 elaborates further on debugmsg syntax.

Table 2-3 *Examining Debugging Messages More Closely*

This Syntax	Tells the WINE Debugger to
-debugmsg warn+dll,+heap	Turn on DLL warning messages and all heap messages
-debugmsg fixme-all,warn+cursor,+relay	Turn off all FIXME messages, turn on cursor warning messages, and turn on all messages relating to API calls
-debugmsg +relay=ADVAPI32	Turns on only those messages which relate to ADVAPI32 code

all

Basic Syntax: ./wine *-debugmsg +all* or *./wine -debugmsg -all*

The argument all causes WINE to generate or disable debugging messages relating to all aspects of the suite's appearance and performance.

advapi

Basic Syntax: ./wine *-debugmsg +advapi* or *./wine -debugmsg -advapi*

When used, the advapi argument enables or disables debugging messages regarding the Advanced Application Program Interface—that is, the API for sophisticated functions such as cryptography and security.

animate

Basic Syntax: ./wine *-debugmsg +animate* or ./*wine -debugmsg -animate*

Supplying the animate argument alerts WINE to debug messages regarding the ANIMATE member of the set of Common controls used in Microsoft-based applications.

aspi

Basic Syntax: ./wine *-debugmsg +aspi* or ./*wine -debugmsg -aspi*

This feature name controls debug messages concerning the *Advanced SCSI Programming Interface (ASPI)*, a standard software interface in the DOS, Windows, OS/2, and Netware environments for SCSI devices. This standard permits the development of drivers and applications that are independent of specific SCSI adapters, and which permit multiple simultaneous access of the SCSI bus by various applications.

atom

Basic Syntax: ./wine *-debugmsg +atom* or ./*wine -debugmsg -atom*

If you need to debug the behavior of named properties of applications running under WINE, this parameter can be of value, since it controls messages regarding such named properties.

bitmap

Basic Syntax: ./wine *-debugmsg +bitmap* or ./*wine -debugmsg -bitmap*

Distorted displays can also be at least partially debugged with the bitmap argument from the command line, since this value controls messaging concerning the use of x/y coordinate bitmaps.

cd

Basic Syntax: ./wine *-debugmsg +cd* or ./*wine -debugmsg -cd*

Since so many GUI-based applications rely heavily on CD-ROM drives, including this debugging parameter when launching WINE can be of value. The parameter controls messaging regarding WINE's manipulating a CD-ROM drive in its role as a data store.

cdaudio

Basic Syntax: ./wine *-debugmsg +cdaudio* or ./wine *-debugmsg -cdaudio*

Just as numerous applications use CDs as data stores, so do many use these devices to augment their presentations with audio. You can facilitate WINE's handling of a CD-ROM drive in its role as an audio presentation device with this debugging channel name.

class

Basic Syntax: ./wine *-debugmsg +class* or ./wine *-debugmsg -class*

Supplying this debugging channel name at the command line causes WINE to present or to forgo presenting debugging information on such categories or classes of screen objects as buttons, scrollbars, and dialogs.

clipboard

Basic Syntax: ./wine *-debugmsg +clipboard* or ./wine *-debugmsg -clipboard*

This debugging channel name, when supplied from the command line, controls WINE's messaging regarding the cut/copy/paste buffer used by GUI-based applications.

clipping

Basic Syntax: ./wine *-debugmsg +clipping* or ./wine *-debugmsg -clipping*

With the clipping parameter, you can control debugging messages concerning the region within an application window that indicates the extent of content to be retained or discarded through cutting or copying.

commctrl

Basic Syntax: ./wine *-debugmsg +commctrl* or ./wine *-debugmsg -commctrl*

Debug the behavior under WINE of common display controls and objects such as tabs, property sheets, and list views by supplying this debugging channel name when launching WINE.

commdlg

Basic Syntax: ./wine *-debugmsg +commdlg* or ./*wine -debugmsg -commdlg*

Debug WINE's handling of common dialogs, that is, windows such as Open and Save, by supplying the commdlg debugging channel name from the command line.

console

Basic Syntax: ./wine *-debugmsg +console* or ./*wine -debugmsg -console*

Enable or disable debug messages regarding DOS console windows under WINE by supplying this debugging channel name at the command line.

crtdll

Basic Syntax: ./wine *-debugmsg +crtdll* or ./*wine -debugmsg -crtdll*

Debug WINE's handling of the Microsoft C runtime library by adding the debugging channel name crtdll to the command line when launching WINE.

cursor

Basic Syntax: ./wine *-debugmsg +cursor* or ./*wine -debugmsg -cursor*

Debug WINE's handling of cursor characteristics and behavior by adding the cursor parameter to the debugmsg run-time option.

datetime

Basic Syntax: ./wine *-debugmsg +datetime* or ./*wine -debugmsg -datetime*

Debug WINE's handling of the Common control called Date/Time—that is, the popup control which manages such things as the switch from daylight savings to standard time—by supplying this debugging channel name at the command line.

ddeml

Basic Syntax: ./wine *-debugmsg +ddeml* or ./*wine -debugmsg -ddeml*

Including this debugging channel name at the command line targets performance problems originating with the *Dynamic Data Exchange Management Library (DDEML)* introduced by Microsoft in Windows 3.1.

ddraw

Basic Syntax: ./wine *-debugmsg +ddraw* or ./*wine -debugmsg -ddraw*

Including ddraw with the debugmsg command-line option targets performance problems originating with applications which rely on Direct-Draw, the display function of DirectX.

dosfs

Basic Syntax: ./wine *-debugmsg +dosfs* or ./*wine -debugmsg -dosfs*

This channel name controls the receipt of debugging messages concerning WINE's handling of the DOS file system.

dosmem

Basic Syntax: ./wine *-debugmsg +dosmem* or ./*wine -debugmsg -dosmem*

The dosmem channel name affects debugging messages regarding allocation and management of memory needed by DOS applications.

dplay

Basic Syntax: ./wine *-debugmsg +dplay* or ./*wine -debugmsg -dplay*

Including this feature name with the debugmsg command-line option targets multi-player capabilities, that is, those that traverse networks, null modem cables, and so on.

dsound

Basic Syntax: ./wine *-debugmsg +dsound* or ./wine *-debugmsg -dsound*

Including the dsound feature name with debugmsg focuses WINE's debugger on performance problems originating with applications which use DirectX sound reproduction facilities.

font

Basic Syntax: ./wine *-debugmsg +font* or ./wine *-debugmsg -font*

Aid the debugging of font-related aspects of WINE's behavior by supplying this channel name at the command line.

gdi

Basic Syntax: ./wine *-debugmsg +gdi* or ./wine *-debugmsg -gdi*

Another channel name useful to debugging display problems is gdi. It relates to WINE's handling of the *Graphical Driver Interface*, a layer found in Win32 code which allows specific drivers to interact with the display aspects of the OS.

global

Basic Syntax: ./wine *-debugmsg +global* or ./wine *-debugmsg -global*

Debug WINE's access to global 16-bit based memory management by supplying this channel name when launching WINE.

heap

Basic Syntax: ./wine *-debugmsg +heap* or ./wine *-debugmsg -heap*

Clearly, in applications as memory-voracious as most GUI-based suites, allocating and freeing memory blocks efficiently is critical. In C, the source language of WINE as well as the Windows interface it recreates, one important aspect of memory management is reliance on the heap, which allows RAM to be assigned and released in an arbitrary yet random manner. So you can help debug poor performance of applications running under WINE by using this channel name.

hotkey

Basic Syntax: ./wine *-debugmsg +hotkey* or ./*wine -debugmsg*
-hotkey

Debug WINE's ability to handle correctly keys or key sequences which have been assigned a specialized function in certain contexts by including this debugging channel name at the command line.

icon

Basic Syntax: ./wine *-debugmsg +icon* or ./*wine -debugmsg -icon*

Debug how, and how well, WINE deals with any graphical symbol which represents a program or process by including the icon channel name when launching WINE.

int

Basic Syntax: ./wine *-debugmsg +int* or ./*wine -debugmsg -int*

Determine WINE's ability to interpret Interrupt Requests (IRQs) correctly by supplying the combination of debugmsg and int at the command line when launching WINE.

int16

Basic Syntax: ./wine *-debugmsg +int16* or ./*wine -debugmsg -int16*

Debug problems associated with IRQ 16, related to control of keyboard behavior such as checking for keystrokes and flushing the keyboard buffer, by supplying the int16 feature name to debugmsg at the command line.

int17

Basic Syntax: ./wine *-debugmsg +int17* or ./*wine -debugmsg -int17*

The IRQ 17 is usually associated with such aspects of control of a printer as initializing a printer port or determining printer status. Therefore, debug printing problems by supplying this channel name when launching WINE.

Int21

Basic Syntax: ./wine *-debugmsg +int21* or ./*wine -debugmsg -int21*

The IRQ 21 relates to reading to and writing from standard input and output. You can debug I/O performance by supplying the int21 debugging channel name at the command line.

Int31

Basic Syntax: ./wine *-debugmsg +int31* or ./*wine -debugmsg -int31*

The specific IRQ 31 is associated with a number of aspects of memory allocation. Therefore, you can help to debug sluggish behavior of applications running under WINE by supplying this channel name at the command line.

ipaddress

Basic Syntax: ./wine *-debugmsg +ipaddres* or ./*wine -debugmsg -ipaddres*

Debug any incorrect use by WINE of the IP Address Common Control by supplying this channel name at the command line.

keyboard

Basic Syntax: ./wine *-debugmsg +keyboard* or ./*wine -debugmsg -keyboard*

Scrutinize WINE's handling of keyboard characteristics and operations with the keyboard debugging channel name.

listbox

Basic Syntax: ./wine *-debugmsg +listbox* or ./*wine -debugmsg -listbox*

Listboxes are display windows which offer a group of possible selections from which one or more may be chosen by the user. You can debug incorrect behavior of such boxes, such as failing to allow the user to make a selection, by adding this channel name to the command line when launching WINE.

local

Basic Syntax: ./wine *-debugmsg +local* or ./*wine -debugmsg -local*

Debug WINE's access to local 16-bit based memory management, that is, to the "local" heap used by 16-bit DLLs and EXEs, by supplying this channel name when launching WINE.

ntdll

Basic Syntax: ./wine *-debugmsg +ntdll* or ./*wine -debugmsg -ntdll*

Debug errors suspected to relate to WINE's reimplementation of the core Windows NT DLL via this channel name.

ole

Basic Syntax: ./wine *-debugmsg +ole* or ./*wine -debugmsg -ole*

Debug any failure in WINE's handling of Object Linking and Embedding (*OLE*) — that is, of the technique common to Windows-based applications which allows them to share the modification of an object — with this channel name.

palette

Basic Syntax: ./wine *-debugmsg +palette* or ./*wine -debugmsg -palette*

Debug how WINE sees and uses the complete range of colors and shades of colors of which a display is capable by supplying this debugging channel name at the command line.

relay

Basic Syntax: ./wine *-debugmsg +relay* or ./*wine -debugmsg -relay*

Investigate the interaction of WINE with the hundreds of calls to APIs which the applications it oversees must make by means of the relay channel name.

Tip

A relay is simply a call to an API. Since supplying this name at the command line when launching WINE causes the suite to display all calls made by any applications running under it into the WINE DLLs, this aptly named channel is also one of WINE's most useful debugging tools. Marcus Meissner and other members of the WINE Project advise that careful reading of the output of -debugmsg +relay, with an eye to those parts of the output which were generated just before a crash or failure, can give real clues to what caused that crash or failure.

thread

Basic Syntax: ./wine *-debugmsg +thread* or ./*wine -debugmsg -thread*

Given the multiple interactions of Windows-based applications with themselves and with various operating system components, the role of threads, that is, of paths or sets of pointers through memory which usually reflect a set of data or instructions associated with a single application, cannot be overemphasized. Supplying this channel name at the command line when launching WINE can therefore be of significant assistance in debugging faulty application performance.

thunk

Basic Syntax: ./wine *-debugmsg +thunk* or ./*wine -debugmsg -thunk*

The term thunking can be applied to any of

- An expression and its variables' values
- In overlay programming, a routine that loads and jumps to the correct overlay
- In Windows programming, a routine or portion of a routine that allows calls between 16- and 32-bit code

In the last context, thunking is heavily used in Windows 95, and is therefore also used by WINE. So, scrutinizing the use of thunking by supplying this channel name at the command line can aid in tracking down the causes of poor application performance.

toolbar

Basic Syntax: ./wine *-debugmsg +toolbar* or *./wine -debugmsg -toolbar*

WINE's presentation and interpreting of Windows-based applications' toolbars can be debugged by supplying this channel name when launching WINE.

toolhelp

Basic Syntax: ./wine *-debugmsg +toolhelp* or *./wine -debugmsg -toolhelp*

Examine how well WINE provides Help for the toolbars presented by the applications it governs with the toolhelp channel name.

tooltips

Basic Syntax: ./wine *-debugmsg +tooltips* or *./wine -debugmsg -tooltips*

Debug WINE's presentation of applications' tool tips by supplying this channel name at the command line when launching WINE.

treeview

Basic Syntax: ./wine *-debugmsg +treeview* or *./wine -debugmsg -treeview*

Not only applications which run under Microsoft's GUI-driven operating systems, but those OSes themselves, rely heavily on a tree view, that is, a flowchart-like representation, of a PC's file system. Debug any problems in the display of such a view by including this channel name at the command line.

vxd

Basic Syntax: ./wine *-debugmsg +vxd* or *./wine -debugmsg -vxd*

A device driver under Windows 3.*x* or 32-bit Windows that is incorporated into and runs as part of the kernel can, as a result, access all memory being used both by the kernel and by all running processes. In addition, such virtual drivers or VXDs have immediate access to hardware, without the need to work through such Windows strata as its Hardware Abstraction Layer or HAL. Debug the Windows applications' use of VXDs, and WINE's handling of this technique, by supplying this debugging channel name when launching WINE.

win16drv

Basic Syntax: ./wine *-debugmsg +win16drv* or *./wine -debugmsg -win16drv*

Examine how well, or poorly, WINE handles 16-bit Windows drivers with the win16drv channel name.

x11

Basic Syntax: ./wine *-debugmsg +x11* or *./wine -debugmsg -x11*

Scrutinize any interaction of WINE with the X Windows System, that is, with the X11 library included in every version of UNIX and Linux, by supplying this channel name at the command line.

Chapter 3

Advanced Compilation and Configuration Issues

DLLs

By using the dll option and appropriate arguments specifying override type and load order, you can control

- Which DLLs will be included in WINE's runtime
- Which types of libraries (built-in, elfdll, native, or special) will be loaded into the address space of a process running under WINE
- The order in which attempts will be made to load the specified libraries

Regarding the first of these conditions, we offer an example of what might at first be considered self-explanatory: the components of WINE's DLL, which accomplishes certain Windows NT–like functions. See Table 3-1.

Table 3-1 *Members of WINE's NT DLL*

This Source File	Accomplishes NT-like
exception.c	Exception handling
file.c	File access
nt.c	Process control
om.c	Object management

Continued

Table 3-1 *Continued*

This Source File	Accomplishes NT-like
reg.c	Registry functions
sec.c	Security functions
sync.c	Process synchronization
time.c	Conversion between time intervals. Among those defined in this file are ticks per second (TICKSPERSEC; equal to 10000000); seconds per hour (SECSPERHOUR); minutes per hour (MINSPERHOUR); days per normal year (DAYSPERNORMALYEAR, or 365), and days per leap year (DAYSPER-LEAPYEAR, or 366)

However, as members of the WINE Project have noted, an administrator, even when knowledgeable about the makeup of a particular DLL, cannot make an arbitrary choice such as "native DLLs are better." Instead, managers must weigh two seemingly contradictory characteristics of the performance of WINE-based applications under different types of DLLs.

Pros of native DLLs

Native DLLs of course guarantee 100 percent compatibility for routines they implement. For example, using the native USER DLL would maintain a virtually perfect and Windows 95–like look for window borders, dialog controls, and so on. Using the built-in WINE version of this library, on the other hand, would produce a display that does not precisely mimic that of Windows 9*x*.

Such subtle differences can be engendered in other important DLLs, such as the common controls library COMMCTRL or the common dialogs library COMMDLG, when built-in WINE DLLs outrank other types in load order.

More significant, less aesthetically oriented problems can arise if the built-in WINE version of the SHELL DLL takes load-order precedence over the native library. SHELL contains routines such as those used by installer utilities to create desktop shortcuts. Since formats for shortcut files are undocumented, WINE did not implement installer routines at the time this book was being written. Therefore, some installers might fail when using WINE's built-in SHELL.

Cons of Native DLLs

Not every application performs better under native DLLs, though. If such a library tries to access features of the rest of the system that are not fully implemented in WINE, the native DLL might work much worse than the corresponding built-in one, if at all. For instance, the native Windows GDI library requires, as you might expect, a Windows display driver, which of course is not present under Intel Unix and WINE. In similar fashion, the native KERNEL DLL simply will not function, since it seeks to access directly the Windows 95 core, once again obviously not present under WINE.

Finally, occasionally built-in WINE DLLs implement *more* features than the corresponding native Windows DLLs. Probably the most important example is the integration of WINE with X provided by WINE's built-in USER DLL. Should the native Windows USER library take load-order precedence, such features as the ability to use the clipboard or drag-and-drop between WINE windows and X windows will be lost.

Deciding between native and built-in DLLs

Clearly, there is no one rule of thumb regarding which load-order to use. The WINE Project advises being familiar with

- What specific DLLs do
- Which other DLLs or features a given library interacts with

and using this information to make a case-by-case decision.

The Project's members state further, however, that for most users, simply staying with the load-order settings specified in the default wine.ini file will suffice.

 Tip

The default load order follows this algorithm: for all DLLs that have a fully functional WINE implementation, or where the native DLL is known not to work, the built-in library will be loaded first. In all other cases, the native DLL takes load-order precedence.

Understanding what DLLs do

The following list briefly describes each of the DLLs whose load order may be modified during the configuration and compilation of WINE.

- ADVAPI32.DLL: 32-bit application programming interfaces
- AVIFILE.DLL: 32-bit application programming interfaces for the *Audio Video Interleave (AVI)* Windows-specific Microsoft audio-video standard
- COMCTL32.DLL: 32-bit shell components
- COMDLG32.DLL: 32-bit common dialogs
- COMM.DLL: 16-bit serial port access
- COMMDLG.DLL: 16-bit common dialogs
- COMPOBJ.DLL: OLE 16-bit component library
- CRTDLL.DLL: Microsoft C runtime
- DCIMAN32.DLL: low-level graphics hardware access
- DDEML.DLL: DDE messaging
- DDRAW.DLL: DirectX drawing libraries

Tip

Direct Data Exchange, or *DDE,* a scheme for interprocess communication, can be seen as a precursor to OLE.

Tip

DirectX, Microsoft's multimedia hardware access software layer, allows C++ code direct access to all multimedia hardware.

- DINPUT.DLL: DirectX input libraries
- DISPLAY.DLL: Display libraries
- DPLAY.DLL, DPLAYX.DLL: Playback libraries for network/multiplayer support
- DSOUND.DLL: DirectX audio libraries
- GDI.DLL: 16-bit graphics driver interface
- GDI32.DLL: 32-bit graphics driver interface
- IMAGEHLP.DLL: 32-bit IMM API help libraries
- KEYBOARD.DLL: Keyboard drivers
- LZ32.DLL: 32-bit LZ file compression

Tip

Lempel-Ziv substitutional, or *LZ*, compression tracks the last bytes of data seen. When LZ compression encounters a phrase it has seen before, it produces a pair of values that represent the position of the phrase in the data buffer and the length of the phrase. LZ compression has been described as moving a sliding, fixed-size window over data.

- LZEXPAND.DLL: File expansion; needed for Windows Setup
- MMSYSTEM.DLL: Core of the Windows multimedia system
- MOUSE.DLL: Mouse drivers
- MPR.DLL: 32-bit Windows network interface
- MSACM.DLL, MSACM.DLL and MSACM32.DLL: Handle Windows audio compression drivers
- MSACM32.DLL: Core of the 32-bit ACM system
- MSNET32.DLL: 32-bit network APIs
- MSVFW32.DLL: 32-bit Windows video system
- MSVIDEO.DLL: 16-bit Windows video system
- OLE2.DLL: OLE 2.0 libraries
- OLE32.DLL: 32-bit OLE 2.0 components
- OLE2CONV.DLL: Import filter for graphics files
- OLE2DISP.DLL, OLE2NLS.DLL: OLE 2.1 16- and 32-bit interoperability
- OLE2PROX.DLL: Proxy server for OLE 2.0
- OLE2THK.DLL: Thunking for OLE 2.0
- OLEAUT32.DLL: 32-bit OLE 2.0 automation
- OLECLI.DLL: 16-bit OLE client
- OLECLI32.DLL: 32-bit OLE client
- OLEDLG.DLL: OLE 2.0 user interface support
- OLESVR.DLL: 16-bit OLE server libraries
- OLESVR32.DLL: 32-bit OLE server libraries
- PSAPI.DLL: PostScript API libraries
- RASAPI16.DLL: 16-bit Remote Access Services libraries
- RASAPI32.DLL: 32-bit Remote Access Services libraries
- SHELL.DLL: 16-bit Windows shell used by Setup

- W32SKRNL: Kernel for Win32 systems
- W32SYS: System libraries for Win32 systems
- WIN32S16.DLL: Application compatibility
- WIN87EM.DLL: 80387 math-emulation libraries
- WINASPI.DLL: ASPI libraries

Tip

The *Advanced SCSI Peripheral Interface (ASPI)*, a set of libraries that provides Windows-based applications with a consistent interface to SCSI devices, has become a de facto standard and is a collection of DLLs that together implement the interface.

- WINDEBUG.DLL: Windows debugger
- WINEPS.DLL: Built-in PostScript printer drivers
- WINMM.DLL: Win32 core multimedia library
- WING.DLL: Early version of accelerated graphics access, that is, predecessor to DirectX
- WINSOCK.DLL: Sockets APIs

Tip

Despite what their name might suggest, sockets are not physical devices. Rather, a socket is the unique combination of a TCP/IP port number and an IP address that identifies every communication handled by the TCP/IP layer. TCP/IP port numbers, in similar fashion, do not indicate physical devices either. Rather, they specify the type of application service, such as e-mail or file transfer, being requested of one TCP/IP machine by another.

- WINSPOOL.DLL: Print spooler libraries
- WNASPI32.DLL: 32-bit ASPI libraries
- WSOCK32.DLL: 32-bit sockets APIs

Experimenting with Load Order

You must follow two rules when attempting to alter the load order of WINE DLLs.

- Always use the same setting for DLL pairs. For example, either both native COMMDLG and COMDLG32 or both built-in versions of these libraries should be specified; don't mix and match with these or any of the other DLLs in the [DllPairs] section of wine.ini.

- If DLL A calls routines of DLL B, and you use the native version of DLL B, you *must* also use the native version of DLL A.

For these DLL pairs

- SHELL/SHELL32
- COMMCTRL/COMCTL32
- COMMDLG/COMDLG32

native versions work quite well: Using native DLLs in these cases has produced noticeable improvements in performance over using the corresponding built-in libraries.

Load-Order Syntax

The remainder of this section sets out sample syntax that can be applied to DLLs whose load order can be specified to WINE.

ADVAPI32

To load the built-in WINE DLL which controls the Advanced API, and therefore affects security, cryptography, and other related functions, but do no more, use this generalized syntax:

```
./wine -dll advapi32
```

To begin by trying to load the native Windows version of advapi32, and, if that effort fails, attempt loading the built-in WINE version of the DLL, use this syntax:

```
./wine -dll advapi32=n,b
```

AVIFILE

This generalized syntax loads the built-in WINE DLL which controls AVI (Microsoft-standard) audio/video functions.

```
./wine -dll avifile
```

This more detailed syntax first tries to load the native Windows version of the AVIFILE DLL, and then the built-in WINE version of that library.

```
./wine -dll avifile=n,b
```

COMCTL32

Loading the built-in DLL that provides access to common 32-bit controls requires this syntax:

```
./wine -dll comctl32
```

Loading the native Windows version of COMCTL32 before trying to load the built-in WINE version of that library follows this syntax:

```
./wine -dll comctl32=n,b
```

COMDLG32

If all you require is to load WINE's 32-bit Common Dialog Library relied upon by many Windows applications, this syntax will suffice.

```
./wine -dll comdlg32
```

If, on the other hand, you seek to ensure smooth performance of those applications by attempting to load the native Windows version of COMDLG32, you'll need this syntax:

```
./wine -dll comdlg32=n,b
```

COMM

Any Windows-based data communications application requires some version of the COMM, or communications, library be compiled into WINE. This syntax supplies the built-in WINE version.

`./wine -dll comm`

Caution

The native Windows versions of COMM don't work with applications running under WINE.

COMMDLG

To specify that the built-in version of the COMMDLG or common dialogs library be loaded into a process's address space, use this syntax:

`./wine -dll commdlg`

To require that the native Windows version of COMMDLG be loaded first, use this syntax:

`./wine -dll commdlg=n,b`

COMPOBJ

To specify that the built-in version of the COMPOBJ, or component object model library, the basis for OLE services, be loaded into a process's address space, use this syntax:

`./wine -dll compobj`

Indicate loading the native Windows version of COMPOBJ first with this syntax:

`./wine -dll compobj=n,b`

CRTDLL

If you want to load the built-in WINE version of the CRTDLL or C runtime library before any other version of this DLL, use this syntax:

```
./wine -dll compobj
```

On the other hand, if you'd like to load the native Windows version of CRTDLL first, use this syntax:

```
./wine -dll compobj=n,b
```

DCIMAN32

To specify that the built-in version of the DCIMAN32 library, which handles display control, be the first version of this DLL which WINE will try to load into a process's address space, use this syntax:

```
./wine -dll dciman32
```

To indicate that the native Windows version of DCIMAN32 be loaded first, use this syntax:

```
./wine -dll dciman32=n,b
```

DDEML

To tell WINE to load its built-in version of the DDEML or Direct Data Exchange messaging library first, use this syntax:

```
./wine -dll ddeml
```

To tell WINE that it should try first to load the native Windows version of DDEML, use this syntax:

```
./wine -dll ddeml=n,b
```

DDRAW

To tell WINE to load its built-in version of the DDRAW or DirectX drawing library before any other version of that DLL, use this syntax:

```
./wine -dll ddraw
```

Caution

WINE cannot work with the native Windows version of this DLL; that version is too heavily hardware-based to allow WINE to do so.

DINPUT

To tell WINE to load its built-in version of the DINPUT or DirectX input library before any other version of that DLL, use this syntax:

`./wine -dll dinput`

Caution

The native version of dinput doesn't work with WINE.

DISPLAY

To specify that WINE should load its built-in version of display libraries before any other means, use this syntax:

`./wine -dll display`

To specify that WINE should try first to load the native Windows version of DISPLAY, use this syntax:

`./wine -dll display=n,b`

DPLAY, DPLAYX

To tell WINE to load its built-in version of the DPLAY (DirectX 2.0) or DPLAYX (DirectX 3.0) multiplayer library before any other version of those DLLs, use one of these syntaxes:

`./wine -dll dplay`
`./wine -dll dplayx`

To tell WINE that it should try first to load the native Windows version of DPLAY or DPLAYX, use one of these syntaxes:

```
./wine -dll dplay=n,b
./wine -dll dplayx=n,b
```

DSOUND

To tell WINE to load its built-in version of the DSOUND or DirectX audio library before any other version of that DLL, use this syntax:

```
./wine -dll dsound
```

Caution

dsound's native version doesn't work with WINE.

GDI

To tell WINE to load its built-in version of the graphics driver interface library before any other version of that DLL, use this syntax:

```
./wine -dll gdi
```

To tell WINE to try first to load the native Windows version of GDI, use this syntax:

```
./wine -dll gdi=n,b
```

GDI32

To tell WINE to load its built-in version of the 32-bit graphics driver interface library before any other version of that DLL, use this syntax:

```
./wine -dll gdi32
```

To tell WINE to try first to load the native Windows version of GDI32, use this syntax:

```
./wine -dll gdi32=n,b
```

IMAGEHLP

To tell WINE to load its built-in version of image help files before any other version of that DLL, use this syntax:

```
./wine -dll imagehlp
```

To tell WINE to try first to load the native Windows version of IMAGEHLP, use this syntax:

```
./wine -dll imagehlp=n,b
```

KEYBOARD

To specify that WINE should load its built-in version of keyboard drivers before any other versions, use this syntax:

```
./wine -dll keyboard
```

 Caution

keyboard's native version doesn't work with WINE.

LZ32

To tell WINE to load its built-in version of 32-bit LZ compression before any other version of that library, use this syntax:

```
./wine -dll lz32
```

To tell WINE to try to load the native Windows version of LZ32 first, use this syntax:

```
./wine -dll lz32=n,b
```

LZEXPAND

To tell WINE to load its built-in version of LZ expansion before any other version of that library, use this syntax:

```
./wine -dll lzexpand
```

To tell WINE to try to load the native Windows version of LZEX-PAND first, use this syntax:

```
./wine -dll lzexpand=n,b
```

MMSYSTEM

Telling WINE to load its built-in version of the core Windows multimedia handlers first requires this syntax:

```
./wine -dll mmsystem
```

Telling WINE to try first to load the native Windows version of MMSYSTEM requires this syntax:

```
./wine -dll mmsystem=n,b
```

MOUSE

To make WINE load its built-in version of mouse drivers, use this syntax:

```
./wine -dll mouse
```

Caution

This DLL's native version doesn't work with WINE.

MPR

To tell WINE to load its built-in version of this 32-bit network interface library before any other, use this syntax:

```
./wine -dll mpr
```

To tell WINE to try first to load the native Windows version of MPR, use this syntax:

```
./wine -dll mpr=n,b
```

MSACM

To tell WINE to load its built-in version of the Microsoft Audio Compression Manager libraries, whether 16- or 32-bit, before any other, use one of these syntaxes:

```
./wine -dll msacm
./wine -dll msacm32
```

To tell WINE to try to load the native Windows version of MSACM or MSACM32 first, use one of these syntaxes:

```
./wine -dll msacm=n,b
./wine -dll msacm32=n,b
```

MSNET32

To tell WINE to load its built-in version of the 32-bit Microsoft network library before any other, use this syntax:

```
./wine -dll msnet32
```

To tell WINE to try first to load the native Windows version of MSNET32, use this syntax:

```
./wine -dll msnet32=n,b
```

MSVFW32, MSVIDEO

To tell WINE to load its built-in versions of either the 32-bit or 16-bit Windows video runtime libraries before any other, use one of these syntaxes:

```
./wine -dll msvfw32
./wine -dll msvideo
```

To tell WINE to try to load the native Windows version of either of these libraries first, use one of these syntaxes:

```
./wine -dll msvfw32=n,b
./wine -dll msvideo=n,b
```

OLE2

To tell WINE to load its built-in version of the OLE 2.0 library before any other, use this syntax:

```
./wine -dll ole2
```

To tell WINE to try to load the native Windows version of OLE2 first, use this syntax:

```
./wine -dll ole2=n,b
```

OLE32

To tell WINE to load its built-in version of the 32-bit libraries for OLE 2.0 before any other, use this syntax:

```
./wine -dll ole32
```

To tell WINE to try to load the native Windows version of OLE32 first, use this syntax:

```
./wine -dll ole32=n,b
```

OLE2CONV

To tell WINE to load its built-in version of import filters for OLE graphics before any other use this syntax:

```
./wine -dll ole2conv
```

To tell WINE to try to load the native Windows version of OLE2CONV first, use this syntax:

```
./wine -dll ole2conv=n,b
```

OLE2DISP, OLE2NLS

To tell WINE to load its built-in version of either the 16- or 32-bit OLE 2.1 interoperability libraries before any others, use one of these syntaxes:

```
./wine -dll ole2disp
./wine -dll ole2nls
```

To tell WINE to try first to load the native Windows version of either OLE2DISP or OLE2NLS, use one of these syntaxes:

```
./wine -dll ole2disp=n,b
./wine -dll ole2nls=n,b
```

OLE2PROX

To tell WINE to load its built-in version of the OLE 2.0 proxy server first, use this syntax:

```
./wine -dll ole2prox
```

To tell WINE to load the native version of OLE2PROX first, use this syntax:

```
./wine -dll ole2prox=n,b
```

OLE2THK

To tell WINE to load its built-in version of the OLE 2.0 thunking library before any other, use this syntax:

```
./wine -dll ole2thk
```

To tell WINE to load the native version of OLE2THK first, use this syntax:

```
./wine -dll ole2thk=n,b
```

OLEAUT32

To tell WINE to load its built-in version of 32-bit OLE automation first, use this syntax:

```
./wine -dll oleaut32
```

To tell WINE to load the native version of OLEaut32 first, use this syntax:

```
./wine -dll oleaut32=n,b
```

OLECLI

To tell WINE to load its built-in version of the 16-bit OLE client first, use this syntax:

```
./wine -dll olecli
```

To tell WINE to load the native version of OLECLI first, use this syntax:

```
./wine -dll olecli=n,b
```

OLECLI32

To tell WINE to load its built-in version of the 32-bit OLE client first, use this syntax:

```
./wine -dll olecli32
```

To tell WINE to load the native version of OLECLI32 first, use this syntax:

```
./wine -dll olecli32=n,b
```

OLEDLG

To tell WINE to load its built-in version of OLE dialogs before any other version of that library, use this syntax:

```
./wine -dll oledlg
```

To tell WINE to try to load the native Windows version of OLEDLG first, use this syntax:

```
./wine -dll oledlg=n,b
```

OLESVR, OLESVR32

To tell WINE to load its built-in versions of either the 16-bit or 32-bit OLE server first, use one of these syntaxes:

```
./wine -dll olesvr
./wine -dll olesvr32
```

To tell WINE to try to load the native Windows version of either of these libraries first, use one of these syntaxes:

```
./wine -dll olesvr=n,b
./wine -dll olesvr32=n,b
```

PSAPI

To tell WINE to load its built-in version of PostScript libraries first, use this syntax:

```
./wine -dll psapi
```

To tell WINE to load the native version of PSAPI first, use this syntax:

```
./wine -dll psapi=n,b
```

RASAPI16, RASAPI32

To tell WINE to load its built-in versions of either the 16-bit or 32-bit Remote Access Services APIs first, use one of these syntaxes:

```
./wine -dll rasapi16
./wine -dll rasapi32
```

To tell WINE to try first to load the native Windows version of either of these libraries requires one of these syntaxes:

```
./wine -dll rasapi16=n,b
./wine -dll rasapi32=n,b
```

SHELL

To load the built-in WINE DLL needed by Windows Setup, but do no more, use this generalized syntax:

```
./wine -dll shell
```

To begin by trying to load the native Windows version of SHELL, and, if that effort fails, attempt loading the built-in WINE version of the DLL, use this syntax:

```
./wine -dll shell=n,b
```

W32SKRNL

To tell WINE to load its built-in version of kernel for Win32 systems first, use this syntax:

```
./wine -dll w32skrnl
```

To tell WINE to load the native version of W32SKRNL first, use this syntax:

```
./wine -dll w32skrnl=n,b
```

W32SYS

To tell WINE to load its built-in version of system libraries for Win32 systems first, use this syntax:

```
./wine -dll w32sys
```

To tell WINE to load the native version of W32SYSfirst, use this syntax:

```
./wine -dll w32sys=n,b
```

WIN32S16

To tell WINE to load its built-in version of the Win32 16- to 32-bit conversion library application computability first, use this syntax:

```
./wine -dll win32s16
```

To tell WINE to load the native version of WIN32S16 first, use this syntax:

```
./wine -dll win32s16=n,b
```

WIN87EM

To tell WINE to load its built-in version of 80387 math coprocessor emulation first, use this syntax:

```
./wine -dll win87em
```

To tell WINE to load the native version of WIN87EM first, use this syntax:

```
./wine -dll win87em=n,b
```

WINASPI, WNASPI32

To tell WINE to load its built-in version of 16-bit or 32-bit Advanced SCSI Peripheral Interface libraries first, use one of these syntaxes:

```
./wine -dll winaspi
./wine -dll wnaspi32
```

To tell WINE to load the native version of either of these libraries first, use one of these syntaxes:

```
./wine -dll winaspi=n,b
./wine -dll wnaspi32=n,b
```

WINDEBUG

To tell WINE to load its built-in version of Windows debugger files before any other versions of these files, use this syntax:

```
./wine -dll windebug
```

To tell WINE to load the native version of WINDEBUG first, use this syntax:

```
./wine -dll windebug=n,b
```

WINEPS

To tell WINE to load its built-in version of enhanced PostScript drivers, use this syntax:

```
./wine -dll wineps
```

Tip

There is no native Windows version of WINEPS.

WINMM

To tell WINE to load its built-in Windows multimedia files first, use this syntax:

```
./wine -dll winmm
```

To tell WINE to load the native version of WINMM first, use this syntax:

```
./wine -dll winmm=n,b
```

WING

To tell WINE to load its built-in graphics drawing utilities first, use this syntax:

```
./wine -dll wing
```

To tell WINE to load the native version of WING first, use this syntax:

```
./wine -dll wing=n,b
```

WINSOCK, WSOCK32

To tell WINE to load its built-in version of 16-bit or 32-bit Windows sockets libraries first, use one of these syntaxes:

```
./wine -dll winsock
./wine -dll wsock32
```

To tell WINE to load the native version of either of these libraries first, use one of these syntaxes:

```
./wine -dll winsock=n,b
./wine -dll wsock32=n,b
```

WINSPOOL

To tell WINE to load its built-in print spooler first, use this syntax:

```
./wine -dll winspool
```

To tell WINE to load the native version of WINSPOOL first, use this syntax:

```
./wine -dll winspool=n,b
```

debugmsg

More specific than its counterpart dll, the debugmsg run time option can be used to produce four categories of error messages that target the behavior of applications running under WINE. Table 3-2 describes those categories or *classes*, as the WINE Project dubs them.

Table 3-2 *Classes of Debugging Messages*

This Class	Produces Messages That
ERR	Relate to serious errors in WINE
FIXME	Relate to behavior of WINE that does not correspond to standard Windows behavior (such as features that have been only partially implemented) and that therefore needs to be improved or fixed
WARN	Relate to unexpected occurrences such as failure to open a file, which do not, however, cause the application or WINE itself to fail
TRACE	Relate to the production of very detailed debugging messages which reflect the line-by-line operation of source code

While any combination of categories of messages is possible, the members of the WINE Project recommend the patterns described in Table 3-3 in specific situations.

Table 3-3 *Uses of Classes of Debugging Messages*

Use the Class(es)	When You Need to Debug
ERR, FIXME, WARN, TRACE	The behavior of a specific component
ERR, FIXME	The behavior of a WINE implementation that is, overall, stable, but that produces intermittent errors or problems
TRACE	The performance efficiency, rather than the performance correctness, of a component

Tip

To paraphrase Commander Uhura in *Star Trek III: The Search for Spock*, be careful what you ask for regarding debugging messages – you may get it. For example, specifying the TRACE class with debugmsg may produce far too much output.

To compile in such a way as to forego debugging messages, and thereby create a WINE executable which is 15% or more smaller than usual, use the syntax outlined in Table 3-4.

Table 3-4 *Precluding Debugging Messages*

Use This Syntax	To Suppress the Production of
./wine -disable - debug	All debugging messages in the classes FIXME, TRACE, and WARN
./wine -disable- trace	All TRACE messages

Tip

Don't be confused by the apparent inconsistent use of case in discussing classes of WINE messages. When working at the command line, supply names such as trace in lowercase. But expect to see them rendered in uppercase when consulting much of the documentation from the WINE project.

Tip

At the time this book was written, the FIXME and ERR message classes were enabled by default, while the TRACE and WARN classes were disabled by default.

Overview of debugmsg command-line syntax

Table 3-5 discusses what, at the time this book was written, was proper generalized syntax for the debugmsg options supplied to WINE from the command line at runtime.

Table 3-5 *Command Line Syntax for debugmsg*

This Parameter	Represents
-debugmsg [yyy] #xxx [,[yyy1]#xxx1]	Debugmsg used with multiple parameters.
[yyy]	The class or classes of messages you wish to produce (e.g., ERR). When not supplied, all classes of messages will be output.
#	Either a plus sign (+), indicating enabling messages, or a minus sign (-), indicating disabling messages.
Xxx	A specific memory buffer, or *channel*, to which messages will be routed. Values for channel must be taken from the list of such names compiled by the WINE project. Only a single such keyword may be supplied with any invocation of debugmsg, but the parameter all may be used to indicate all debugmsg channels.
[,[yyy1]	Additional, optional message classes.
#xxx1]	Additional, optional message channels.

Tip

Understand the term channel to be synonymous with component of WINE, or what we've called feature names. Note that no spaces should appear after the comma that must separate such names. However you think of it, a name can represent either a complete DLL or a single API. Names must be supplied to WINE at startup with the same spelling and in the same case as they appear in WINE's list of such names, in turn created during compilation.

How to use debugmsg efficiently

Quite probably, only developers need or can achieve an in-depth understanding of the output produced by the debugmsg configuration option.

Why, then, is this option the subject of so much of this chapter? There's one simple reason: It is the principal tool for debugging the compilation of WINE. As a result, administrators must grasp its output's meaning, if only to the extent of that output's providing clues to the WINE Project for further modifications of WINE's source. Think of it this way: Much as Microsoft engages in an ongoing process of debugging its products, based upon the thousands of bug reports it receives and as bug fixes available on its Web site demonstrate, so WINE's developers need clues from administrators, testers, and users in order to improve WINE. The remainder of this section presents hints regarding users' understanding debugmsg output in a way that will allow them to contribute to the enhancement process by submitting informative bug reports.

Re-run with -debugmsg +relay

Let's use the ubiquitous Solitaire as an example. Should WINE crash while running this program, the command

```
wine -debugmsg +relay sol.exe > why_crash
```

would produce extensive diagnostic output pertaining specifically to sol.exe.

Tip

In the example just given, we've redirected debugmsg's output to a file called why_crash precisely because that output can be so large. debugmsg frequently produces several megabytes.

In this context and continuing with our effort to debug the WINE/Solitaire interaction, another useful command is

```
echo quit|wine -debugmsg +relay sol.exe >& why_crash;
tail -n 100 why_crash > why_crash_precis
```

Tip

This second example not only redirects debugmsg's output but also then takes only the last hundred lines from the end of the initial output file, in order to create diagnostics of more manageable size.

Note that these commands will be supported by all shells under which WINE runs. Note also that the final report file produced in this way will contain, in those last hundred lines of debugging output, information such as register dumps and backtraces, critical to programmers' correcting the problem at hand. As a result, the WINE Project asks that this information not be deleted, even if it is meaningless to you.

Provide thorough information in bug reports

As the text at the URL http://www.winehq.com/source/documentation/bugreports puts it, this means we need more information than a simple *MS Word crashes whenever I run it. Do you know why?*

The WINE Project suggests that bug reports include at least

- The version of WINE being run. This information can be produced by the command

  ```
  wine -v
  ```

- The operating system under which WINE is running. Include distribution and version.

- The compiler and version under which WINE's runtime was produced. This information can be obtained with the command

  ```
  gcc -v
  ```

- The version of Windows installed on your machine.

- The application you're trying to run under WINE. Include version number, and, if the software was downloaded from the Internet, the URL from which the application was obtained.

- The command-line syntax you used to start WINE.

- Any other information you think may be relevant or helpful, such as X server version if, for instance, you're encountering problems with X.

Once you've compiled this information, post it to the Usenet newsgroup comp.emulators.ms-windows.wine. In your post, also include report files such as those created with commands like

```
echo quit|wine -debugmsg +relay sol.exe >& why_crash;
tail -n 100 why_crash > why_crash_precis
```

debugmsg command-line syntax

The remainder of this section presents specific syntax examples for the debugmsg configuration option. Note that we haven't included either TRACE or FIXME in this section, since we feel these classes of messages to be of significance primarily to developers rather than administrators. But we do offer generalized examples of debugging that can be applied to all the channel or feature names WINE understands. We also close the section with a complete list of those names.

- Enable all messages for a channel: wine -debugmsg +*channel name*
- Disable all messages for a channel: wine -debugmsg -*channel name*
- Enable all error messages for a channel: wine -debugmsg err+ *channel name*
- Disable all error messages for a channel: wine -debugmsg err-*channel name*
- Enable all fixme messages for a channel: wine -debugmsg fixme+ *channel name*
- Disable all fixme messages for a channel: wine -debugmsg fixme-*channel name*
- Enable all warning messages for a channel: wine -debugmsg warn+*channel name*
- Disable all warning messages for a channel: wine -debugmsg warn-*channel name*
- Enable all trace messages for a channel: wine -debugmsg trace+*channel name*
- Disable all trace messages for a channel: wine -debugmsg trace-*channel name*
- Enable all messages for all channels: wine -debugmsg +*all*
- Disable all trace messages for all channels: wine -debugmsg -*all*

Tip

It bears repeating. The keyword all represents not only all classes of messages, but also all feature or channel names known to WINE.

WINE Channel Names

Table 3-6 presents the most significant of the channel names specified by the WINE project as of the time this book went to press.

Table 3-6 *Summarizing WINE Channels*

Channel Name	Role
All	All channels, all categories of debugging messages.
Advapi	Advanced Application Program Interface (e.g., cryptography, security).
Animate	ANIMATE common control.
Aspi	Advanced SCSI Programming Interface.
Atom	Named properties of application.
Bitmap	X/Y coordinate bitmaps.
Cd	CD-ROM drive in its role as a data storage device.
cdaudio	CD-ROM drive in its role as an audio presentation device.
class	Categories of screen objects (e.g., scrollbars, dialogs).
clipboard	Cut/copy/paste buffer.
clipping	Region within a window containing text to be retained or discarded.
commctrl	Common display controls (e.g., property sheets, list views).
commdlg	Common dialogs (e.g., Open and Save windows).
console	DOS console window.
crtdll	Microsoft C runtime library.
cursor	Cursor characteristics and behavior.
datetime	Common control of same name.
dc	Device Content memory structure (i.e., display's x/y origin, coordinates, etc.).
ddeml	Dynamic Data Exchange Management Library of Windows 3.x.
ddraw	DirectDraw, the display feature of DirectX.
dosfs	DOS file system.
dosmem	DOS applications' memory management.
dplay	DirectPlay, the feature of DirectX controlling multiplayer and network game support.
dsound	DirectX sound reproduction.
font	Font display.
gdi	32-bit Windows' Graphical Driver Interface.

Continued

Table 3-6 *Continued*

Channel Name	Role
global	16-bit applications' memory management.
heap	Allocation and release of RAM.
hotkey	Special-purpose keystrokes or keystroke sequences.
icon	Application and system icons.
int	All interrupt requests.
int10	IRQ 10 (i.e., control of display mode).
int16	IRQ 16 (i.e., control of keyboard and keyboard buffer).
int17	IRQ 17 (i.e., printer control).
int21	IRQ 21 (i.e., reading from/writing to standard input/output).
int31	IRQ 31 (i.e., memory allocation.
io	Overall input and output.
ipaddress	IP Address common control.
keyboard	Keyboard characteristics (e.g., default language).
listbox	Listbox common control.
listview	Listview common control.
local	16-bit-based memory management.
midi	Musical Instrument Digital Interface; hardware specification and protocol used to communicate note and effect information between computers, music keyboards, synthesizers, etc. Essentially, a high-speed serial connection which distinguishes between input and output. The basic unit of information includes a note number which represents pitch, and a key velocity which indicates volume.
mmaux	Auxiliary multimedia channels.
mmio	Multimedia input and output.
msacm	Audio compression drivers.
ntdll	Core Windows NT DLL.
ole	Object Linking and Embedding.
progress	Applications' progress bars.
reg	Registry.
region	Area on-screen display.
relay	Call to an API.
segment	Memory management.

Channel Name	Role
sem	Semaphores (common method for restricting access to shared resources in multi-processing environments. A semaphore is a variable that can be accessed only for specific purposes such as testing or incrementing. What's more, while such processes are active, no other process may access the semaphore in question).
static	Memory management; specifically, static variables.
statusbar	Applications' status bars.
stress	Memory management.
thread	Memory management; specifically, sets of pointers through memory pertaining to a single application's data or instructions.
thunk	Interoperability between 16- and 32-bit code. Of particular use, therefore, in dealing with Windows 95 applications.
toolbar	Applications' toolbars.
toolhelp	Applications' Help for tools.
tooltips	Applications' mouse-over tips for tools.
treeview	Treeview common control.
vxd	Applications' use of virtual drivers and the resultant immediate access to hardware.
wing	Windows graphics-drawing utilities.
winsock	Windows sockets APIs.
x11	Interaction with the X Windows system.
x11drv	Drivers for the X Windows system.

Other Debugging Tools

This section discusses other tools that might assist in debugging the compilation of WINE.

WINE's built-in debugger

WINE includes its own debugger, which recognizes even such source-code esoterica as segmented and flat addresses, Unix and Windows symbol tables, and more. The debugger may be invoked in either of two ways.

You may use the -debug option at WINE's command line. For example,

```
wine -debug sol.exe
```

would cause WINE to invoke its debugger before beginning running Solitaire.

An operating system command line such as

```
kill -HUP 12345
```

where 12345 is the process ID of WINE, obtained from the OS command ps, will automatically start the debugger.

OS utilities

A pair of operating system utilities may also be of some value in debugging WINE's compilation.

file

This standard Unix/Linux utility recognizes file types, among them DOS and Windows executables, and outputs small amounts of information about them.

binfmt_misc

binfmt_mis is a Linux kernel patch which recognizes DOS, Windows, and even Java executables in their native formats. binfmt_misc is available as a patch to Linux 2.0.*x*, and is integrated into kernel versions 2.1.43 and later.

Configuration Files

This section discusses, not typical WINE configuration file entries, but techniques appropriate to certain areas of such files.

Fonts

Fine-tuning fonts under WINE is a several-step process, only the last step of which involves modifying the WINE configuration file wine.conf. However, in order to do that correctly, one must first accomplish its prerequisites.

Converting Windows fonts

Within the tools directory of many X Windows implementations is a utility called fnt2bdf.

fnt2bdf doesn't need root access. All you need do is

1. Supply it with the name or names of the font files to be converted; the utility will translate those fonts to X Windows encoding

2. Redirect that encoding into a file whose name ends in the extension .bdf

Tip

Here's a generalized example of using fnt2bdf.

```
fnt2bdf some.fon > some.bdf
```

Use this utility to convert bitmap fonts — that is, those whose file names end in the extension .FON, such as SERIFE.FON, COURE.FON, and ROMAN.FON, into X Windows format. Follow these steps:

1. Extract bitmap fonts by running fnt2bdf.

2. Convert .bdf files produced in this way into .pcf files by running the companion utility bdftopcf.

Table 3-7 describes some of the options with which bdftopcf can be run.

Table 3-7 *bdftopcf Options*

Option	Use
-pn	Sets font glyph padding, allowing each glyph in the font to have each scanline padded to one, two, four, or eight bytes
-un	Sets font scanline unit, which can describe the size of the unit of data to be swapped; units can be one, two, or four bytes
-m	Sets font bit placement order to most-significant-bit-first
-l	Sets font bit placement order to least-significant-bit-first
-t	Causes bdftopcf to convert fonts to terminal fonts if possible (In terminal fonts, each glyph image is padded to the same size. Such fonts can therefore be rendered quickly.)
-l	Causes fonts whose glyph images do not fill the bitmap image, that is, whose pixels do not extend to fill the area defined for them, to have their placement recomputed by bdftopcf
-o output-file	Causes bdftopcf to write its output to a file rather than to its default destination, standard output

Tip

bdftopcf, a font "compiler" that frequently acts as a font format conversion utility, can convert font files from the Bitmap Distribution Format to the Portable Compiled Format. The latter format can be read by several hardware architectures while at the same time allowing the specification of a particular architecture that can read font files directly, without any reformatting. Such a scheme improves performance on the specified machine, while ensuring at the same time that font files will remain portable.

3. Copy all .pcf files you create in this way to the appropriate directory on your server, in most cases /usr/lib/X11/fonts/misc.

Tip

Be aware that on most Linux systems you'll need to be the superuser to carry out this copy.

Tip

Alternately, you can create a new font directory for your converted fonts. But if you do, be sure to add that new directory's name to the font path.

4. Run the additional X related utility mkfontdir on the directory to which you copied .pcf font files.

Tip

mkfontdir creates an index of a directory's X font files. Here's a generalized example of its use.

```
mkfontdir directory-name
```

For each directory name that you supply as an argument, mkfontdir reads all font files, searching for properties named FONT or for the name of the file minus its extension. Any such items mkfontdir finds it then converts to lowercase and uses as font names, which, together with the name of the corresponding font file, are written to the file fonts.dir in the directory specified as a command line argument. The X server and font server then can use fonts.dir to locate font files. Particular font files read by mkfontdir include PCF, SNF, and BDF. Should the same font be present in several formats, mkfontdir will first choose PCF.

5. Finally, run the X utility xset to make your X server aware of the new fonts. Use the specific syntax xset fp rehash.

Tip

xset is a utility that allows you to establish user display-related preferences under X.

Table 3-8 describes the xset utility.

Table 3-8 *Understanding xset*

Option	Role
-display server	Specifies an X server.
-b	Controls bell volume, pitch, and duration; accepts up to three numerical parameters, a preceding hyphen (-), or an on/off flag. If no parameters are supplied at the command line, or the on flag is used, X will use system defaults. If the hyphen or off indicators appear, the bell will be turned off. If you supply only one numerical parameter, bell volume will be set to that value, which is taken to represent a percentage of the maximum possible volume. A second numerical parameter must be used in order to specify bell pitch, and is taken to represent hertz. Any third numerical parameter specifies the duration of bell in milliseconds.
-c	Controls key click. Like -b, can take a value, a preceding hyphen, or an on/off flag. No argument, or the on flag, indicates using system defaults. The hyphen, or the off flag, specifies disabling keyclick. Any value from 0 to 100 indicates volume of keyclick as a percentage of the maximum possible.
-fp= path	Sets the font path to the indicated path. Paths are interpreted by the X server, not by the client.
-fp rehash	"Resets" the font path to its current value, causing the server to reread the font databases in the current font path.
-m	Controls mouse parameters such as acceleration and threshold. The former can be specified as an integer or a fraction, causing a mouse or other pointing device to move acceleration times as fast when it travels more than the threshold number of pixels.
-p	Controls pixel color values.
-r	Controls autorepeat of keystrokes.

Continued

Table 3-8 *Continued*

Option	Role
-s	Sets screen-saver parameters. Accepts as many as two numerical parameters, a blank/noblank flag, an expose/noexpose flag, an on/off flag, an activate/reset flag, or a default flag. With either no arguments or the default flag, system reverts to default screen-saver characteristics. on or off turn screen-saving on or off. activate flag forces activation of screen-saving even if it had previously been turned off. reset forces deactivation of screen-saving. blank causes blanking the display rather than showing a screen-saving background; noblank does the inverse. Expose allows the server to discard window contents; noexpose tells the X server to disable screen-saving unless the server can regenerate screens without causing warnings.
-q	Supplies information on the current X server settings.

Editing wine.conf

Once font files have been converted and identified in the way just described, you must edit the configuration file wine.conf, removing aliases for any fonts so created and installed.

Tip

Be aware that while WINE doesn't require such fonts, its look and feel can be improved by fonts that the X server with which it runs prefers.

Tip

Some applications try to load custom fonts as they launch; Word 6.0 for Windows is one such app. As a result, WINE may display a message of this sort.

```
STUB: AddFontResource( SOMEFILE.FON )
```

Simply convert any font files indicated in such messages, by the method just discussed. This additional conversion will also help prevent the failure of fnt2bdf to convert unidentified bitmap fonts. Note also that even this additional conversion will not cause such messages to go away, but will induce WINE to work around the problem by using extracted fonts such as the hypothetical SOMEFON.

Tip

TrueType fonts aren't as easily rendered. Although there are several commercial applications that can convert them, the quality of the results is far from stellar according to members of the WINE Project, who suggest, as an alternative, using a font server capable of rendering TrueType fonts.

Adding, rather than removing, font aliases in wine.conf

Many Windows applications assume that fonts included in original Windows 3.1 distribution are always present. By default, WINE creates a number of aliases that map such fonts to existing X fonts: Table 3-9 outlines these font aliases.

Table 3-9 *WINE Font Aliases*

Windows Font	Maps to X Font
MS Sans Serif	-adobe-helvetica-
MS Serif	-bitstream-charter-
Times New Roman	-adobe-times-
Arial	-adobe-helvetica-
System	No mapping or alias

Because WINE does not automatically map the System font, and because of the scenario previously noted in which applications may install at runtime, there may be occasions on which you will have to use the technique described in the section "Converting Windows Fonts." Should such conversion fail for any reason, you have an alternative. You can force the font mapper to choose as closely related as possible an X font, by adding an alias to the [fonts] section of wine.conf. A generalized example of such an entry might look like this.

```
AliasN = Windows font name, X font name
```

In this syntax, the indicator N represents an integer indexed from 0 (zero). Therefore, if you defined two such font aliases in wine.conf, they would be, respectively, Alias0 and Alias1.

A more specific example follows.

```
Alias0 = System, -international-
```

Tip

Before you make any aliasing additions to wine.conf, be sure that the X font to which your edits refer actually exists. Use the X utility xfontsel, a program which can display the names of all fonts known to your X server, to examine samples of each, or retrieve the full name for a font.

Once such aliasing takes place, WINE will depart from its normal font substitution process. Ordinarily, WINE's font mapper translates X font names into Windows-comprehensible font names quite sensibly. For instance, the X font -adobe-helvetica- would be translated simply as Helvetica. But when an alias has been supplied in wine.conf, the alias will replace the font name to which WINE would otherwise have mapped the font in question. So, for example, the line

```
Alias0 = Arial, -adobe-times-
```

would cause WINE to replace applications' Arial font with something other than its normal substitute.

Tip

However font conversion and aliasing are carried out, WINE will ignore font aliases if it determines that a correct native X font is available.

Cached font metrics

WINE stores detailed information about available fonts in the file ~/.wine/.cachedmetrics. Should you wish to house this file in a different area of the overall file system, copy it to the desired destination directory, and then add a line of this type to the [fonts] section of wine.conf.

```
FontMetrics = full path name of the metrics file
```

Tip

WINE uses its font metrics file to rebuild font dimensions from scratch when it detects changes in the X font configuration.

Inappropriately sized fonts

Some Windows applications specify height in pixels when requesting that a font be rendered. Translating such requests to pixels is not easy. No single point-to-pixel ratio exists; conversion factors depend on the real physical size of a display.

The X system tries to estimate that size, but can err. To correct problems of inappropriately sized fonts that might be due to such erroneous estimates, add an entry like the following to the [fonts] section of wine.conf:

```
Resolution = some integer
```

In general, higher numbers give you larger fonts, but you'll have to experiment. The WINE Project recommends values in the range 60–120 as a good place to start.

Printing

As work on this book was beginning, the WINE Project had established a means of identifying Windows 3.x — that is, 16-bit — printer drivers to WINE. The method once again involves editing wine.conf. You must follow these steps:

1. Add the line

   ```
   printer=on
   ```

   to the [wine] section of wine.conf.

2. You may also have to add the following to the [TrueType] section of win.ini.

   ```
   TTEnable=0
   TTOnly=0
   ```

Spooling

The [spooler] section of wine.conf maps a port such as LPT21 to a file or a command via a pipe. For example, consider the following lines.

```
LPT1:=somethin.ps
LPT2:=|lpr
```

As a result of these lines, the first printer port would be associated solely with the driver file somethin.ps, while the second such port would be equivalent to a pipe to the command lpr.

Problems can arise with such a scheme when a job is sent to an unlisted port. In such situations, a file is created with that port's name. For instance, if an application tried to print to something called LPT3, a file called LPT3: would be created automatically. However, if that file has not been identified to WINE, spooling to it may fail.

Another Configuration Tool

TkWine is a set of two scripts, the first a desktop for WINE, and the second a setup program. This latter script, TkWineSetup, is, like its peer, written in TCL and intended to facilitate the process of installing or compiling WINE. TkWineDesktop attempts to make WINE more user-friendly by supplying a desktop that allows you to display icons in the left pane and set application in the right pane.

Both these scripts were, at the time this book was being prepared, still alpha, with TkWineDesktop described as extremely so, but still useful for setting applications' WINE-related options.

TkWine can run on any Linux or other Intel Unix machine which has the package Tcl76/Tk41 or higher. TkWine makes calls only to basic shell commands.

Tip

If you intend to try TkWine to configure WINE for development work, you may also need wget and ftp to carry out downloads and cvs updates, as well as, of course, make for compilation.

Tip

TkWine is available for download at `http://panter.soci.aau.dk/ ~dailywine/tkwine/`. But be aware that, as this book was going to press, work on TkWine had been put on hold, and was expected to remain so for at least several months.

Part II

Advanced Configuration Issues

Chapter 4

Interoperability and Interconnectivity Issues

Interoperability Issues

In order better to understand the hurdles presented to interoperability in heterogeneous environments, we will, in this section, examine two models for such interoperability, both based upon strategies put forward by Microsoft. These strategies are directly reflected in the interoperability tools available to WINE.

Four-layer model

In one version of its interoperability strategy, Microsoft divides its model into four layers: network, data, applications, and management. It refers to this four-part model as NDAM. NDAM is characterized by techniques intended to evolve, rather than replace all or parts of, information technology infrastructures.

Network interoperability

Microsoft defines network interoperability as the ability for multi-vendor systems to communicate with each other using common protocols. In this category, the company includes a number of features.

Protocols Microsoft operating systems and Microsoft-compatible applications support a wide range of protocols, including

- TCP/IP
- IPX/SPX
- SNA
- Dynamic Host Configuration Protocol (DHCP)
- Domain Name Service (DNS)
- Internetworking Protocols such as RIP, the Router Information Protocol

Tip

Many students of networking and internetworking consider RIP a limited and outdated method of controlling routing. Other routing protocols such as the Border Gateway Protocol (BGP) and the Open Shortest Path First or OSPF protocol are considered less limited.

Terminal Access Through its SNA Server for 3270 and 5250, as well as through the TN3270 and TN5250 protocols, Microsoft offers its implementation of standard tools for providing access to remote hosts as an emulated terminal of those hosts.

Print services Applications' ability to make use of networked and remote printing resources makes up one of the most significant interoperability issues. Microsoft's support for interoperable print services relies not only on existing protocols but also on some still under development, such as the Internet Printing Protocol.

Data interoperability

Microsoft defines the second layer of its interoperability model as the capacity to allow users and applications to access and query information stored in individual or multiple data sources. It further divides this layer into three categories.

File system In accomplishing access for users to administrative information regarding files, such as that offered by Novell or Unix network file servers, Microsoft relies primarily on native protocols such as IPX/SPX and NFS.

Database Microsoft carries out access to data stored in heterogeneous databases, and the ability to query such mixed, multiple data stores, by means of various data translation technologies, as well as by database interoperability drivers such as ODBC.

E-mail Citing messaging systems as the storage medium for much data in heterogeneous environments, Microsoft further cites its reliance on standards such as the Simple Mail Transfer Protocol (SMTP), the Internet Mail Access Protocol (IMAP4), and the Post Office Protocol (POP3) as its tools for providing interoperability in this area.

Applications

In presenting the idea of applications interoperability, Microsoft refers to the need to ensure that new applications in a client/server environment can interoperate with existing applications and data.

Presentation services In proposing a seamless interface for applications in heterogeneous environments, Microsoft has only the use of browsers and HTML to offer.

Transactions As in so many other areas of its interoperability model, Microsoft relies primarily upon standards-based tools such as the XA and TIP protocols to provide applications the ability to take part in transactions across multiple, dissimilar systems.

Components To offer applications the ability to incorporate modules not running under Windows, Microsoft suggests the use of the COM programming model, as well as the use of third-party software.

Management

Microsoft sees management interoperability as the streamlining of the administration of multiple systems, and in particular of user accounts on such systems.

Security Working toward the goal of accomplishing security through user authentication, Microsoft has been developing technology to provide single sign-ons and password synchronization among Microsoft operating systems and such platforms as Unix, NetWare, and the IBM AS/400. In addition, Microsoft supports such standards as Kerberos.

Directory Directory interoperability—that is, a single, consistent system for naming, accessing, and managing networked file systems—is accomplished in the Microsoft model through such standards as the Lightweight Directory Access Protocol (LDAP) as a means of synchronization with Novell's Network Directory Services (NDS).

Systems management In offering tools for managing multiple, heterogeneous operating environments, Microsoft relies on the Simple Network Management Protocol (SNMP), as well as on the development by third-party vendors of other management architectures.

Five-layer model

Another Microsoft model for interoperability differs slightly from the first in both the number of layers which it presents and in how it allocates specific functions to those layers. This second model, of interest primarily to developers, consists of

- Network connectivity services such as directory services
- Information access constructs such as messaging, file-sharing, and print sharing
- Cross-platform management
- Application interoperability, including access to relational databases
- Distributed cross-platform application development

As was the case with Microsoft's four-tier interoperability model, this latter scheme presages interoperability tools available to WINE.

The Primary Interoperability Tool

Given Microsoft's heavy use of existing standards in its interoperability models and WINE's need to allow Microsoft-based applications to run under Intel Unix in a variety of environments, the remainder of this chapter describes the most significant interoperability tool available to WINE today. That tool is Samba, a suite which in turn relies upon the Server Message Block or SMB protocol. All discussion of Samba that follows is in the context of a local area network consisting primarily of Windows-based clients, but also containing at least one Intel Unix machine acting as a WINE platform.

The SMB protocol

This section describes SMB and provides basic installation and configuration instructions for Samba, perhaps the most widely used implementation of that protocol.

Understanding SMB

All versions of Windows for Workgroups, Windows 95, Windows 98, and Windows NT can run SMB as a client, a server, or both. This means that any such system can, through SMB, share files, printers, serial ports, and even such virtual data communications entities as named pipes.

SMB operates as a client/server, request/response protocol, meaning that the client, by initiating exchanges with requests to the server, is in effect in control of such exchanges.

 Tip

One exception exists to this rule of thumb. If a client requests a file in a locked mode, and the responding server, after granting that request, receives a subsequent request for the same file from another client, the original lock will be broken by the server, and an unsolicited message sent to the client informing it of the broken lock.

Servers make file systems and other resources (printers, mailslots, named pipes, APIs) available to clients on the network. Client computers may have their own hard disks, but they also want access to the shared file systems and printers on the servers.

SMB, like so many other internetworking entities, requires clients to connect to servers using TCP/IP, NetBEUI, or IPX/SPX.

Tip

Should they operate in TCP/IP environments, SMB clients must actually use NetBIOS over TCP/IP to make their initial connection.

Through this initial connection, clients send commands called server message blocks to the server in order to interoperate with remote file systems over networks.

Tip

When either TCP/IP or NetBEUI makes the initial SMB connection, it is the NetBIOS API that actually does the work. Microsoft refers to such connections as both NBT and NetBT in others, and calls NetBEUI-based SMB connections NBF.

Since both its TCP/IP and NetBEUI forms rely on the NetBIOS API, SMB must also very frequently employ NetBIOS names. Such names can be up to 15 characters long. Most frequently, these names simply represent the computer running NetBIOS. However, some implementations of NetBIOS, including Microsoft's, also require that these names be in uppercase, especially when presented to servers as the CALLED NAME.

SMB security

SMB offers two levels of security.

Share security Security measures directed at a server's shares, consisting primarily of share passwords which provide access to all files within a share, are

- SMB's initial security model
- The only security available in NetWare's Core and CorePlus protocols
- The default form of security of both Windows for Workgroups and Windows 95

User security SMB also offers security applied to individual files, and based on user rights. Under user level security, every user must log on to an SMB server and be authenticated by that server. When the user has been authenticated, the client from which he or she has connected receives a user ID (UID) which it must present on any subsequent attempts to connect to the server.

SMB requests and responses

For both requests and responses, server message blocks must contain a header of a fixed size, followed immediately by parameter and data sections, both of which may be of varying sizes.

After connecting at the NetBIOS level, an SMB client can request services from its server. However, doing so requires that client and server first identify which protocol variant each is using. To accomplish this, the client sends an SMB to the server, listing the protocol dialects that it understands. The server responds with the index of the dialect that it wants to use, or 0xFFFF if none of the dialects the client informed it of was acceptable.

When a client/server conversation is fully established, a number of other actions can be taken by the client. Table 4-1 outlines these.

Table 4-1 *Initial SMB Client Actions*

Client Action	SMB Required	Server Response
logon to the server	sesssetupX SMB	indicates whether or not client has supplied a valid username password pair, as well as a UID for the logged on user
connect to a tree	tcon or tconX SMB specifying the network name of the share to which client wishes to connect	indicates the ID that the client will use in all future SMBs relating to that share
open a file	open SMB	indicates that the requested file has been opened
read a file	read SMB	indicates that the requested file has been opened in read mode
write to a file	write SMB	indicates that the requested file has been opened for modification
close a file	close SMB	indicates that the requested file has been closed by the server

Samba

Samba, an SMB server freely available from more than 30 mirrored download sites, which in turn can be reached from **www.samba.org,** was developed by Andrew Tridgell and is maintained by programmers around the world. Samba runs on many of the same Intel Unix variants that support WINE, including Linux, Solaris, and NetBSD. In these environments and more, Samba offers the NT LM 0.12 protocol dialect, allowing it to participate in

Windows NT-based domains as either a Primary Domain Controller (PDC) or a member. Particularly in the latter role, Samba can both browse and be a browse master. In addition, from a domain, Samba can process logon requests from Windows 95 systems.

Tip

Microsoft has a number of SMB server implementations for the Windows operating system spectrum. These are not separate products, however, but instead are integrated into the version of Windows in question. Despite this integration, these Microsoft SMB servers can be switched off though the Control Panel or at the command line, in the latter case with the command `net stop server`.

Tip

Windows 95's and Windows NT's SMB servers react differently to some of the same sequences of SMBs. Members of the Samba project have concluded from this that Microsoft bases each of these servers on its own unique source code.

Installing Samba

Following are the steps for obtaining and installing Samba. Note that the commands illustrating this process rely upon one another, and should therefore be executed in the sequence given below.

1. Download the source code from `www.samba.org` to a temporary directory such as /tmp.

2. Make a directory at a convenient point in the file system, and copy the source into this directory. Sample commands:

   ```
   mkdir -p /home/source/samba
   cd /home/source/samba
   cp /tmp/samba-2.0.3.tar.gz
   ```

3. Unzip and extract the source. Sample commands:

   ```
   gunzip samba*
   tar xvf samba*
   ```

4. Change to the directory created by tar.

   ```
   cd samba-2.0
   ```

5. Configure the compilation process for your system. Sample commands:

```
cd source
./configure
```

6. Compile the source code.

```
make
```

7. Install the compiled code.

```
make install
```

Sequences such as the one just outlined install all Samba files in directories under /usr/local/samba, with binaries in /usr/local/samba/bin and man pages in /usr/local/samba/man.

 Tip

Note that Samba's default home in the file system, /usr/local/, also houses WINE. Keep this in mind when anticipating how much free disk space installing Samba in addition to WINE will require.

Configuring Samba

Following are the initial steps needed to configure Samba.

1. Modify your system's search path to allow it to find the Samba man pages.

```
MANPATH=$MANPATH: /usr/local/samba/man
```

2. Reboot to allow the change in search path to take effect.

3. Create the Samba lock directory.

```
mkdir /usr/local/samba/lockdir
```

4. Create the Samba configuration file: /usr/local/samba/lib/smb.conf.

A basic configuration file should contain lines like these:

```
# Global parameters
workgroup = SOMEGRP
guest ok = Yes
security = Share
read only = No
hosts allow = localhost, 192.123.4.
```

```
hosts deny = All
[redhat]
comment = Red Hat Linux 6.0
path = /
```

Note the following regarding smb.conf:

- Text like `# Global parameters`, a comment line, and `[redhat]`, a section header, should appear at the beginning of lines.

- All other lines should begin with a tab character.

- Replace SOMEGRP in the example above with the name of a Windows workgroup. On a Windows 95 system, this name appears on the Identification tab of the Network icon of Control Panel.

- Replace `192.123.4` in the example above with the first three components of the IP addresses used on your network.

- Retain the period after the partial IP address in the configuration file: it is a required indicator.

Tip

Like WINE, Samba indicates all section headers in its configuration file with square bracket pairs ([ ]).

This sample Samba configuration file provides for

- Clients accessing a Red Hat platform from Windows machines on the local network

- No password being required of such clients

- The Red Hat machine's root file system being shared

- Incoming connections to the Red Hat PC having default user and group IDs of nobody

Tip

Further changes to smb.conf, such as those needed to provide sharing of specific directories, the use of passwords, and printing, are best accomplished by means of the Samba utility called swat.

To verify that smb.conf has been created correctly, use a command sequence like this one:

```
cd /usr/local/samba/bin
./testparm
```

As a result, you should see a display similar to this:

```
Load smb config files from /usr/local/samba/lib/smb.conf
Processing section "[redhat]"
Loaded services file OK.
Press enter to see a dump of your service definitions
```

At this point, press Enter to see more detail, or Ctrl C to leave the test utility.

Autostarting Samba

Most of Samba's services originate with one of three daemons.

- smbd, the Samba server, which handles incoming connections on TCP port 137
- nmbd, the NetBIOS name server, which handles incoming connections on TCP port 139
- swat, a Web-based Samba configuration tool that handles incoming connections on TCP port 901

Tip

swat, a scaled-down Web server, responds to HTTP connections on port 901. swat provides a graphical interface for configuring Samba and for some of Samba's documentation. To connect to swat, just start your browser and point it at http://localhost:901.

A Samba server's underlying operating system needs to tell its Internet daemon (*inetd*) to start the appropriate Samba daemon whenever a request arrives at any of these ports. Table 4-2 outlines what must be done to so advise inetd.

Table 4-2 *Setting up Samba's Daemons*

Action	Sample Command(s)

Edit /etc/services.	Immediately after the line that appears similar to:
	
	`somerpc     111/tcp      rpcbind`
	insert the lines:
	
	`netbios-ns   137/udp    # Samba nmbd`
	`netbios-ssn  139/tcp    # Samba smbd`
	Immediately after the lines that appear similar to:
	
	`ldaps      636/udp     # LDAP protocol`
	`over TLS/SSL (was sldap)`
	insert the line:
	
	`swat      901/tcp    # Samba swat`

Edit /etc/inetd.conf.	Add the following three lines to the end of the internet daemon's configuration file.
	
	`netbios-ssn  stream tcp  nowait root`
	`/usr/local/samba/bin/smbd smbd`
	
	`netbios-ns   dgram udp  wait  root`
	`/usr/local/samba/bin/nmbd nmbd`
	
	`swat      stream tcp  nowait.400   root`
	`/usr/local/samba/bin/swat swat`

Tell inetd to re-read its configuration file.	`pkill -HUP inetd`

Testing Samba

Testing Samba for basic functionality is simplicity itself. Use Windows Explorer on a client to examine Network Neighborhood. If you've installed and configured Samba correctly, you should see an entry for your Intel Unix machine there. What's more, you should be able to

- Browse the file system on that machine from the Windows PC
- Copy files that have global read access from the Intel Unix machine to the Windows PC by means of drag-and-drop
- Copy files from the Windows PC to any directories with global write permissions on the Intel Unix machine

smb.conf in more detail

smb.conf houses Samba runtime configuration information. The remainder of this section describes the file's format and possible parameters.

> **Tip**
>
> This section helps you understand smb.conf. But don't expect to be using the information here from the command line too often. smb.conf was designed to be modified by means of swat.

smb.conf format Like WINE's wine.conf, the Samba configuration file contains sections, which are in turn made up of parameters and their associated values. Sections must begin with the name of the section set out within square brackets. Sections are seen to continue until the next such section header is encountered.

Sections contain lines in this form.

```
parameter = value
```

Every line in smb.conf, whether section header, parameter/value, or comment, must end in a newline character.

Neither section nor parameter names are case sensitive. Whitespace before or after an equals sign (=) in a parameter/value line is ignored, as are leading, trailing and internal whitespace in section and parameter names, and leading and trailing whitespace in parameter values. However, internal whitespace in parameter values is interpreted literally.

Any line in smb.conf which begins with a semicolon (;) or a pound sign (#) is ignored, as are lines containing only whitespace. Samba understands any line ending in a backslash (\) as continuing to the next physical line.

Values assigned to parameters must be either strings, which require no encasing quotation marks, or Boolean values, which may be rendered as

- yes/no
- 0/1
- true/false

Boolean-valued parameters ignore case in their values. String-valued parameters, however, preserve case.

Ordinary smb.conf sections Except for the [global] section, every section in smb.conf describes a single shared resource, or share. Thus, the section name also functions as the name by which the share is known under Samba. Shares most frequently consist of

- A file or print to which access is being granted
- A description of the access rights available to the user of the share

Tip

Sections, and therefore shares, may be set up as guest services, which require no password, but rather rely on a server OS guest account to define access privileges. In any case, a Samba server cannot grant more access than its host OS permits.

Sample smb.conf section/share definitions The sample below sets up a shared file subsystem, defining its path and its means of access.

```
[bigdir]
path = /usr/leila/publicstuf
writeable = true
```

The next sample section defines a printable, but read-only, share, indicating that the only write access permitted is that which is needed to open, write to, or close a spool file. Here, guest ok permits access as the default (guest) user.

```
[printdir]
path = /usr/spool/public
read only = true
printable = true
guest ok = true
```

Special sections smb.conf recognizes three special sections:

- **Global:** Parameters in this section apply to the server as a whole, or are defaults for sections which do not specifically define certain items.

■ **Homes:** Should smb.conf include a section called [`homes`], services connecting clients to their home directories can be created on the fly by the server. When connection requests are made, smb.conf's other sections are scanned. If a match with a section header is found, the corresponding section is used. If no match is found, the requested section name is treated as a user name and looked up in the local password file. If the name exists and the correct password has been given, a share is created by duplicating the information in the [homes] section. Two modifications are then made to the newly created share:

- The share name is changed to the located username

- If no path was given, the path is set to the user's home directory

Here's an example of a sensible [homes] section.

```
[homes]
writeable = yes
```

■ **Printers:** If the Samba configuration file contains a [printers] section, users can connect to and print from any printer specified in the local host's printcap file. When a client makes a request to connect to a printer, the configuration file's existing sections are scanned. If a match with a section header is found, the corresponding section is used. If no match is found, but a [`homes`] section exists, that section will be used as just described. Otherwise, the requested section name is treated as a printer name and the appropriate printcap file is scanned to see if the requested section name is a valid printer share name. If a match is found, a new printer share is created by duplicating the [printers] section. A few modifications are then made to the newly created share:

- The share name is set to the located printer name

- If no printer name was given, the printer name is set to the located printer name

- If the share does not permit guest access and no username was given, the username is set to the located printer name

A typical [`printers`] section might look like this.

```
[printers]
path = /usr/spool/public
writeable = no
guest ok = yes
printable = yes
```

Tip

If guest access is specified in the [homes] section, all home directories will be visible to all clients, *without a password*. Therefore, should such access be configured, it should be accompanied by the specification of read-only mode.

Parameter values and substitution Many smb.conf parameter values can be specified by means of substitution identifiers. Some frequently used substitution identifiers are

- %a: architecture of the remote machine; may include Samba, WfWg, WinNT, and Win95.
- %d: process id of the current server process.
- %H: home directory of the current service.
- %h: Internet hostname under which Samba is running.
- %I: IP address of the Samba client.
- %L: NetBIOS name of the Samba server.
- %M: Internet name of the client.
- %m: NetBIOS name of the client.
- %N: name of NIS home directory server. If you have not compiled Samba with the -with-automount option then this value will be the same as %L.
- %p: path of the service's home directory; obtained from NIS auto.map entry.
- %P: root directory of the current service.
- %R: selected protocol level after protocol negotiation; can be any of CORE, COREPLUS, LANMAN1, LANMAN2 or NT1.
- %S: name of the current service.
- %T: current date and time.
- %U: session user name.
- %u: user name of the current service.
- %v: Samba version.

Name mangling Samba supports what it calls name mangling, which allows clients to use file names that don't conform to the classic 8.3 model. Through name mangling, Samba can also adjust the case of 8.3 filenames. Several options control name mangling. All of these options can be set per service or globally.

- **Mangle case:** determines whether names containing characters not of the default case will be mangled

- **Case sensitive:** determines whether filenames will be case sensitive

- **Default case:** controls whether new file names will be represented in upper- or lowercase

- **Preserve case:** controls whether the names of new files are created with case passed from the client, or are forced to be the default case

- **Short preserve case:** can be used with preserve case to permit long filenames to retain their case, while rendering short file names as lower case

Tip

By default, Samba 2.0, like Windows NT server, is case-insensitive but case-preserving.

User name and password validation A Samba server takes these steps, in the indicated sequence, to decide if it will allow a connection to a specified service that an application running under WINE might request. Only if all the steps fail is a connection request denied. Conversely, when a step passes, any steps following it will not be taken. And finally, if a service has been identified as guest only = yes, Steps 1 to 5 below will be ignored.

1. If the client has forwarded a user name and password that can be validated by the system's password programs to the Intel Unix system, the connection is made under that username.

2. If the client has previously registered a username with the Intel Unix system and now supplies a correct password for that username, the connection is allowed.

3. Should neither Steps 1 or 2 succeed, the client's NetBIOS name and any user names it may previously have employed are checked against the supplied password. With a match, the connection is allowed as the corresponding user.

4. Should none of Steps 1, 2, or 3 succeed, but

   • The server had previously validated a user name and password pair for the client

   • The client has passed a validation token appropriate to that user name and password

   the connection will be allowed under the validated user name.

 Tip

Should the appropriate section in smb.conf contain a line of the form

```
revalidate = yes
```

Samba will skip Step 4 in attempting to validate users.

5. If

   • A user = parameter/value pair exists in the appropriate section of smb.conf

   • The client has supplied a password

   • That password matches any of the user names defined in user=

   the connection will be made under the matched user name.

 Tip

Names in the user= list that begin with an at sign (@) expand to a list of users in the group of the same name.

6. If the service has been defined as a guest service, a connection will be made under the user name given for the service by the guest account = parameter/value pair.

Service parameters available to validated user sessions Table 4-3 outlines what we consider the most important Samba configuration parameters pertaining to services available to applications like those running under WINE.

Table 4-3 *Service-Related Samba Parameters*

Parameter	Applied	Defines	Default	Example
admin users	to specific sections	List of users who will be granted administrative, that is, superuser, privileges on the share	None	Admin users = bob
allow hosts	to specific sections	Comma, space, or tab delimited set of hosts which can access a service. Can be defined by host name or IP address.	None	Allow hosts = pjb, 123.45.6
announce as	globally	type of server nmbd will announce itself as, to a network neighborhood browse list	Windows NT; valid options are NT, Win95, WfW	Announce as = WFW
announce version	globally	Version numbers (major and minor) nmbd uses to announce itself as a server	4.2	Announce version = 2.0
auto services	globally	list of services that will be added to browse lists	None	Auto services = odo kira nog
available	to specific sections	Service enabling or disabling	Yes	Available = no
bind interfaces only	globally	Limitations on the interfaces on a machine that will serve smb requests	False	Bind interfaces only = true
blocking locks	to specific sections	Behavior of smbd when clients request byte range locks on a region of an open file	True	Blocking locks = false

Continued

Table 4-3 *Continued*

Parameter	Applied	Defines	Default	Example
browse list	globally	Availability of a browse list to a client from smbd	Yes	Don't change this setting.
browseable	to specific sections	Appearance of a share in list of available shares	Yes	Browseable = no
case sensitive	globally	case sensitivity or lack thereof on Samba's part	No	Case sensitive = yes
change notify timeout	globally	Ability of client to tell server to monitor a particular directory for changes, and only to reply to SMB requests when such changes have taken place; specified in units of seconds	60	Change notify timeout = 300
character set	globally	Ability of smbd to map incoming filenames from a DOS to several built in Unix character sets	Empty string	Character set = ISO8859-1
client code page	globally	DOS code page or character set clients accessing Samba use.	Default for MS-DOS, Windows 95, and Windows NT: 437. default for these OSes' Western European releases: 850.	Client code page = 123
comment	to specific sections	label text associated with a share when a client queries the Samba server for available shares	No comment string	Comment = PJB's Stuff

Parameter	Applied	Defines	Default	Example
config file	globally	file Samba will substitute for the default smb.conf	smb.conf	Config file = /usr/ local/samba/lib/ anothr.conf
copy	to specific sections	Duplication of service entries	None	Copy = original service name
create mask	to specific sections	Mask for files. Any bit/mode not set will be excluded from access permissions defined for a file when it is created.	0744	Create mask = 0775
deadtime	globally	Number of minutes of inactivity before a connection is considered dead. A deadtime of zero indicates that no auto-disconnect is permitted.	0	Deadtime = 15
debug timestamp	globally	Timestamping of Samba log messages	Yes	Debug timestamp = no
default service	globally	Name of a service which will be connected to if the service actually requested cannot be found	None	Default service = spool
delete readonly	to specific sections	Permission for readonly files to be deleted	No	Delete readonly = yes
deny hosts	to specific sections	Hosts that cannot access services. Specified as either host name or IP address.	None (i.e., no hosts specifically excluded)	Deny hosts = 123. 456.7. dcnet.dccc.edu

Continued

Table 4-3 *Continued*

Parameter	Applied	Defines	Default	Example
directory mask	to specific sections	Modes, specified as octal, and used when converting DOS modes to Unix modes when creating Unix directories. Any mode not set here will be excluded from the access permissions defined for a directory when it is created.	0755	Directory mask = 0744
domain logons	globally	Samba server satisfying Windows 95 or 98 domain logons	No	Domain logons = yes
dont descend	to specific sections	Directories that the server should always show as empty	None (i.e., Samba may descend all directories)	Dont descend = /home/sybase, /dev
dos filetime resolution	globally	Manner in which reported system time will be rounded down to nearest two-second boundary when a query call that requires one-second resolution is made to smbd	False	Dos filetime resolution = true
dos filetimes	to specific sections	Modification of timestamps on files	False	Dos filetimes = true
follow symlinks	to specific sections	Ability of smbd to follow symbolic links in a share prevented or permitted	No	Follow symlinks = yes

Parameter	Applied	Defines	Default	Example
force group	to specific sections	Name used as default group for all users connecting to the service	None	Force group = trekgroup
force user	to specific sections	Name used as default user for all users connecting to this service	None	Force user = tb
fstype	to specific sections	String that specifies type of filesystem a share will use	NTFS	Fstype = Samba
guest account	to specific sections	Username for accessing services defined as guest services	Specified at compile time. Usually nobody.	Guest account = guestuser
guest ok	to specific sections	Need for a password in order to connect to the service	No	Guest ok = yes
guest only	to specific sections	Permission for or prevention of guest connections to the service	No	Guest only = yes
hosts equiv	globally	Name of a file to read for the names of hosts and users requiring no password	None	Hosts equiv = /etc/hosts.equiv
invalid users	to specific sections	Users that cannot connect to the service	None	Invalid users = bilbo frodo sam @hobbits
keepalive	globally	Number of seconds server will wait before assuming a client session is inactive	0	Keep alive = 60
load printers	globally	Loading or failing to load all printers listed in /etc/printcap for browsing	Yes	Load printers = no

Continued

Table 4-3 *Continued*

Parameter	Applied	Defines	Default	Example
lock directory	globally	Directory where lock files reside	/tmp/samba	Lock directory = /usr/local/samba/lockdir
locking	to specific sections	Willingness on Samba's part to satisfy clients' lock requests	Yes	Locking = no
log file	globally	Name of Samba log file	None	Log file = /usr/local/samba/log
logon home	globally	Directory assigned to client when a Windows 95, 98, or NT Workstation logs onto a Samba Primary Domain Controller. Allows commands like NET USE H: /HOME to be run.	\\%N\%U	Logon home = \\pjb2\%U
logon path	globally	Directory where roaming profiles reside	\\%N\%U\ profile	Logon path = \\ PROFILESRVR\HOME \%U\PROFILE
logon script	globally	file containing commands to be downloaded and run on the client when a user successfully logs in	None	Logon script = \\scripts\%U.bat
lppause command	to specific sections	Command to be executed on the server to stop printing or spooling a specific print job	None	Lppause command = /usr/bin/lphalt %p-%j -p0
lpq command	to specific sections	Command to be executed on the server to obtain printer status information	None	Lpq command = /usr/bin/lpq %p

Parameter	Applied	Defines	Default	Example
lpresume command	to specific sections	Command to be executed on the server to restart or continue printing or spooling a specific print job	None	Lpresume command = /usr/bin/lphalt %p-%j -p2
lprm command	to specific sections	Command to be executed on the server to delete a print job	None	Lprm command = /usr/bin/cancel %p-%j
mangled names	to specific sections	Willingness of Samba to map to DOS-compatible names, and make visible under Unix, non-DOS names	Yes	Mangled names = no
mangling char	to specific sections	Character used in name mangling	~	Mangling char = ^
map hidden	to specific sections	Ability of Samba to grant the global execute bit to DOS hidden files	No	Map hidden = yes
map system	to specific sections	Ability of DOS system files to receive the global execute bit	No	Map system = yes
max connections	to specific sections	Maximum simultaneous connections to a service	0	Max connections = 10
max log size	globally	Maximum size Samba's log file will be allowed to attain. Specified in kilobytes.	5000	Max log size = 1000
maxopenfiles	globally	Maximum number of open files one smbd file serving process may have open simultaneously for a given client	10000	Maxopenfiles = 9000

Continued

Table 4-3 *Continued*

Parameter	Applied	Defines	Default	Example
max xmit	Globally	Maximum packet size Samba will negotiate. Values below 2048 can cause problems.	65535	Max xmit = 9216
message command	globally	Command the Samba server will run when it receives a WinPopup style message	No message command	Message command = csh &
netbios aliases	globally	lList of NetBIOS names that nmbd will advertise as additional names by which the Samba server is known	No names	Netbios aliases = SAMBA1 SAMBA2
null passwords	globally	Ability of clients to access accounts with null passwords	No	Null passwords = yes
only user	to specific sections	Ability of Samba to preclude or allow connections with user names not in Samba's user list	False	Only user = true
os level	globally	Level Samba advertises itself as for browse elections	32	os level = 65 (guaranteed to beat out any NT Server)
panic action	globally	Command from operating system to be called when either smbd or nmbd crashes	Empty string	Panic action = /usr/ scripts/panic_script
password server	globally	Remote SMB server where Samba will do all its name and user password validation	Empty string	Password server = NT-PDC, NT-BDC (where BDC stands for *Backup Domain Controller*)

Parameter	Applied	Defines	Default	Example
path	to specific sections	Directory or directories that the user of the service may access	None	Path = /usr/pjb_2
preexec	to specific sections	Command to be run whenever the service is connected to	None (no command executed)	Preexec = echo \"%u connected to %S from %m \" > /tmp/log
preserve case	to specific sections	Creation of new filenames with the case that the client passes, or with the default case	Yes	Preserve case = no
print command	to specific sections	Command to be used to process a spool file	Default printing command of your Intel Unix implementation	Print command = /usr /local/samba/bin/ prints
printcap name	globally	Ability of Samba to override the compiled-in default printcap name	None	Printcap name = /etc/ newprintcap
printer	globally	Name of the printer to which spooled print jobs will be sent	None	Printer name = laserdoodle
protocol	globally	Level of protocol that is the highest supported by the Samba server	NT1	Protocol = LANMAN1
read list	to specific sections	List of users who have only read-only access to a service	Empty string	Read list = lb, genardi
root directory	globally	Directory to which the Samba server will change its root directory on startup	/	Root directory = /wine
security	globally	Manner in which clients respond to Samba. One of the most important settings in smb.conf.	USER	Security = DOMAIN

Continued

Table 4-3 *Continued*

Parameter	Applied	Defines	Default	Example
smb passwd file	to specific sections	Path to the encrypted smbpasswd file	Compiled in	Smb passwd file = /usr/samba/smbpasswd
smbrun	globally	Path to the smbrun binary	Compiled in	Smbrun = /usr/local/samba/bin/smbrun
status	globally	Ability of Samba to log connections to a status file	Yes	Status = no
time server	globally	Ability of nmbd to advertise itself as a time server to Windows clients	False	Time server = true
username	to specific sections	List of users which will serve as the basis for testing the supplied password. Password tested in turn, from left to right, against each name in the list.	Guest , or the name of the service	Username = spock, sarek, tuvok, vorek, @vulcans
valid chars	to specific sections	Characters that the Samba server should consider valid in file names	A reasonable set of valid characters for English systems	Valid chars = 0345: 0305 0366:0326 0344 :0304 (e.g., to allow filenames to contain Swedish characters)
valid users	to specific sections	Users who may log onto a service	No list; i.e., anyone can log on	Valid users = greg, dharma, @sitcom
wide links	to specific sections	Willingness of the Samba server to follow links in the Intel Unix file system	Yes	Wide links = no
wins server	globally	IP address or DNS name of the WINS server with which nmbd must register	None	Wins server = 192.9.200.1

Parameter	Applied	Defines	Default	Example
wins support	globally	Ability of nmbd to act as a WINS server	No	Don't change this setting.
workgroup	globally	Workgroup the Samba server will appear in when queried by clients	Set at compile time to WORKGROUP	Workgroup = NEWGROUP
write list	to specific sections	Ability of users specified in list to access a service in both read and write modes	Empty string	Write list = root, @others

Chapter 5

Interoperability in More Detail

Samba-Based Interoperability

Whether as a vehicle for

- Allowing Windows-based PCs to access applications running under WINE on a Linux server
- Allowing Intel Unix machines to run Microsoft applications presented by Windows servers
- Providing interoperability that complies with the Microsoft model

Samba stands as the best candidate for WINE's interoperability partner. This chapter expands upon using Samba in this context.

Sharing a Linux drive with Windows machines

Configuring Samba to allow Windows machines access to Linux drives and through them to WINE can be done entirely through editing the Samba configuration file smb.conf. For example, to share a directory with all users would require modifications to smb.conf like those below.

```
[public]
comment = For All Users
```

```
path = /home/pub
public = yes
writable = yes
```

These edits would make the file subsystem in question accessible for both reading and writing to any user who can connect to the Samba server. To maintain general readability but limit the ability to modify to a specific user group would require slightly different edits to smb.conf, such as those that follow.

```
[public]
comment = For All Users
path = /home/pub
public = yes
writable = yes
write list = @engineering
```

For all versions of Windows prior to

- Windows 98
- Windows NT 4.0 with Service Pack 3 or higher
- The most recent versions of Windows 95

such a section in smb.conf would suffice. However, in the aforementioned Microsoft OSes, encrypted passwords are the default. Samba, on the other hand, defaults to unencrypted passwords. Therefore, because Samba cannot make connections anonymously, it cannot immediately provide for browsing servers when either the client or server involved employs encrypted passwords. Should you receive a message such as

```
You are not authorized to access that account from this
machine.
```

when trying to connect to a Microsoft platform in order to browse it, there's a good chance that such an encrypted/unencrypted password mode mismatch exists. In such cases, you can either

- Configure your Samba server to use encrypted passwords
- Configure its Windows clients to use unencrypted passwords

Configuring Windows 9x for unencrypted passwords

Setting up unencrypted passwords on a Windows 9x machine may be a necessary step in allowing that machine access to WINE through a Samba server. To do so, make the following addition to the Registry with the registry editor regedit.

1. Access the key HKEY_LOCAL_MACHINE\System\ CurrentControlSet\Services\VxD\VNETSUP.

2. Add to this key the parameter/value pair

   EnablePlainTextPassword Data   0x01

Caution

As Microsoft's documentation itself often advises, editing the Registry must be done with great caution if serious damage to a system is to be avoided.

Configuring Windows NT for unencrypted passwords

To set up unencrypted passwords on a Windows NT machine, make the following addition to the Registry with regedit.

1. Create the new registry entry HKEY_LOCAL_MACHINE\System\ CurrentControlSet\Services\Rdr\Parameters

2. Add to this new entry the parameter/value pair

   EnablePlainTextPassword Data   0x01

Configuring Samba to use encrypted passwords

Should your environment require Samba to use encrypted passwords in order for it to act as a means of connecting to WINE, you must add lines like those shown below to the [global] section of smb.conf.

```
encrypt passwords = yes
smb passwd file = /etc/smbpasswd
```

Once such edits have been made and both the client and the server machines involved have been rebooted, your initial connection to the Samba server must include the name of the share you wish to browse in either of the following formats.

```
\\<remote host name>\<share name>
\\<remote host IP address>\sharename
```

You may need to set a number of other parameters in order to ensure that your Samba server presents file names to its grabbag of Windows clients in a familiar way. Table 5-1 outlines these parameters and their applicability.

Table 5-1 *Fine-Tuning File Name Presentation Under Samba*

This Parameter/Value Pair	Should Be Set Here
mangle case = yes	Windows 9x and NT
case sensitive = no	Samba server
default case = lower	Samba server
preserve case = yes	Samba server
short preserve case = no	Samba server

Sharing a Linux printer with Windows machines

Before you can configure Samba to allow Windows machines to access and share a Linux printer made available through WINE, you must, of course, first ensure that the printer works properly under Linux. Assuming that is the case, you must then

1. Add lines like those that follow to smb.conf

   In the [global] section:

   ```
   [global]
   printing = bsd
   printcap name = /etc/printcap
   load printers = yes
   log file = /var/log/samba-log.%m
   lock directory = /var/lock/samba
   ```

   In the [printers] section:

   ```
   [printers]
   comment = All Printers
   ```

```
security = server
path = /var/spool/lpd/lp
browseable = no
printable = yes
public = yes
writable = no
create mode = 0700
```

In sections governing specific printers:

```
[printjet]
security = server
path = /var/spool/lpd/lp
printer name = lp
writable = yes
public = yes
printable = yes
print command = lpr
```

Tip

Be sure that whatever path you define for a specific printer matches that defined for it in /etc/printcap.

Tip

The lines

```
printcap name = /etc/printcap
load printers = yes
```

control the default loading of all printer definitions stored in /etc/printcap. Should your smb.conf contain these lines, you need not set up printers individually.

2. Ensure that, for every Windows account name and password that may attempt to access a Linux printer under Samba, an equivalently named account exists on the Linux box.

Table 5-2 elaborates on this name/password correspondence requirement.

Table 5-2 *Effect of User Accounts on Accessing Printers Under Samba*

	Correct Usage	Incorrect Usage
User Name on Windows Machine	harry_p	betty
Printer Name	\\newsrvr\newptr	\\newsrvr\newptr
Linux Machine Name	\newsrvr	newsrvr
User Name on Linux Machine	harry_p	No account, or one such as *bettie*
Effect	The user neelix will be able to supply his or her name and password at the Windows machine in order to access the Linux box and its printer.	The user will be unable to access the Linux box and its printer.

Sharing a Windows drive with Linux machines

Samba provides client as well as server capabilities: an SMB client that offers an ftp-like interface from the command line is included with the Samba distribution. This utility can easily be used to transfer files between a Windows server and a Linux client, thus enabling that client to work on those files with an application running under WINE.

To see, from a Linux client, which shares are available on a Windows host, use this command

```
/usr/sbin/smbclient -L host name
```

of course replacing *host name* with the name of the machine whose resources you wish to browse. Executing this command returns a list of service names, each of which represents a drive, portion of drive, or printer that the Windows machine is willing to share with you.

At this point, if the Windows-based SMB server has any security configured, you'll be asked to provide a password. In response to this request, you may use either

- The password for a guest account
- Your own password on the Windows server

To use the SMB client to access, rather than simply list, remote services, type this form of the command.

`/usr/sbin/smbclient` *service name password*

Once again, be sure to substitute

- The actual name of the file subsystem or printer you wish to access, for the parameter *service name*
- A valid password on the remote Windows machine, for the parameter *password*

 Tip

Remember that you're running such a command from a Linux box and may therefore need to escape – that is, cause to be passed over rather than executed – some characters that Linux views as metacharacters with special meaning. So, for instance, the command

`/usr/sbin/smbclient \\sharedstuf\public`
`a_password`

while syntactically correct from the Windows server's point of view, would have to be rendered as

`/usr/sbin/smbclient \\\\sharedstuf\\public`
`a_password`

in order to cause Intel Unix to ignore, rather than carry out the symbolic function of, the backslash.

After connecting to the remote Windows Samba server, you'll next see Samba client login information and prompts, like those below.

```
Server time is Tue Dec 07 17:47:54 1999
Timezone is UTC+10.0
Domain=[WORKGROUP] OS=[Windows NT 4.0] Server=[NT LAN
Manager 4.0]
smb: \>
```

> **Tip**
>
> The Samba organization recommends the smbfs package as a more effective alternative to smblient. smbfs provides two utilities, smbmount and smbumount, which function in exactly the same way as their Intel Unix namesakes. smbfs accompanies most recent Linux distributions but requires that you compile smbfs support into your kernel.

Sharing a Windows printer with Linux machines

Take these steps to share a printer on a Windows machine with Samba clients running WINE.

1. Ensure that entries in the client's /etc/printcap reflect the printing-related directory structure on the Windows machine.

2. Ensure that the script /usr/bin/smbprint is available on the client. smbprint appears in the Samba source, but not in all Samba binary distributions.

3. Should you need to convert ASCII files to Postscript, as, for example, when the latter is the only type printer available, your Samba client must also have access to nenscript, a Postscript converter most frequently found in /usr/bin.

Configuring browsing

Whichever side of the Microsoft/Intel Unix fence your Samba clients and servers sit on, effective interoperability and interaction with WINE depend in large part upon how you've configured browsing.

The Role of WINS

While it plays a critical role in the resolution of NetBIOS names to IP addresses, the *Windows Name Service* or *WINS* has little direct involvement with the handling of browse lists under Samba. That is true for a number of reasons:

- Windows networking, like Samba, relies on SMB messaging, implementing that messaging strictly by means of NetBIOS.

- Samba implements NetBIOS by encapsulating it over TCP/IP.

- In either case, NetBIOS-based networking uses broadcast messaging for browse list management.

- Under Samba, that is, under NetBIOS over TCP/IP, this broadcast messaging uses UDP messages, which can be either broadcast or unicast.

This combination of circumstances results in

- The remote announce parameter in smb.conf being called upon to send browse announcements to remote network segments via unicast UDP

- The remote browse sync parameter of smb.conf carrying out browse list collation using unicast UDP

Also as a result of this combination of circumstances, in cases in which Samba is the only SMB server present, the Samba organization recommends setting up the utility nmbd on *one machine only*, to act as a WINS server. Such singular configuring

- Simplifies browsing management

- Precludes situations in which the configuration of one Samba WINS server for every network segment in turn requires the use of the remote announce and remote browse parameters in every smb.conf file on that segment, in order to accomplish intersegment browsing

Tip

Since browse lists are essentially a collection of broadcast messages that repeat at intervals of about 15 minutes, establishing a reliable browse list may require as much as 45 minutes, especially if that list must span network segments.

The Remote announce parameter

To force the recognition on a remote network or segment of all local NetBIOS names, smb.conf uses the remote announce parameter.

Two forms of generalized syntax for this parameter appear below and are elaborated upon in Table 5-3.

```
remote announce = 1.2.3.4, or 1.2.3.255
```

or

```
remote announce = 1.2.3.4/WORKGROUP, or 1.2.3.255/WORKGROUP
```

Table 5-3 *Remote Announce Syntax*

The Parameter	Represents	And Might Be Replaced By
1.2.3.4 or 1.2.3.255	either the Local Master Browser or LMB IP address, or the broadcast address of the remote network	192.345.6.78, or 192.345.6.255 where the netmask is assumed to be 24 bits, that is, 255.255.255.0
WORKGROUP	the optional designation of either the client's workgroup or the workgroup on the remote network	the actual workgroup name

Tip

Using the remote workgroup name at this point can cause NetBIOS names to appear to belong to that workgroup and therefore may also cause name resolution problems. As a result, the Samba organization discourages this type of use.

Tip

Another drawback of the remote announce parameter is that, since it uses the broadcast address of the remote network, every host on that network receives its announcements. However much a waste of bandwidth this might seem, it is sometimes unavoidable when the IP address of the remote LMB is unavailable.

The remote browse sync parameter

smb.conf uses the remote browse sync parameter to announce to an LMB that its NetBIOS name list must be synchronized with the Samba LMB's browse list. This technique works *only* if the Samba server so configured is also the LMB on its network segment.

Generalized syntax for remote browse sync is

```
remote browse sync = 1.2.3.4
```

where 1.2.3.4 is either the IP address of a remote LMB or the network broadcast address of a remote segment.

Using WINS

As a means of expediting name resolution across interoperating environments such as those that include WINE, the Samba organization recommends using either Microsoft or Samba WINS. WINS makes interoperability more efficient in a number of ways.

Client receives a list of all machine names that can offer the NetLogon service from WINS, thereby reducing broadcast traffic and speeding up logon processing.

WINS forces the synchronizing of browse lists across all LMBs. Further, WINS helps LMBs to coordinate their browse lists with the domain master browser or *DMB* by identifying that DMB.

Tip

The term domain master browser as used in this context refers not to a Windows NT Domain but rather to the master controller for browse list information. As such, WINS can play this role only in workgroups, and not across NT domains.

Of critical importance to this technique is the requirement that the TCP/IP stack on every client be configured to use a WINS server. Any client not set up in this way will continue to use only broadcast-based name registration. As a result, not only will unnecessary network traffic be generated, but WINS also may never recognize or service these broadcasts. However it might take place, machines that have not registered with a WINS server will fail name-to-address mapping and will therefore generate access errors.

To configure Samba as a WINS server, add this line to the [globals] section of smb.conf:

```
wins support = yes
```

To configure Samba to register with a WINS, add a line of this form to the [globals] section of smb.conf.

wins server = 1.2.3.4

Tip

Never use both wins support = yes *and* wins server = 1.2.3.4 simultaneously if the indicated IP address is that of the local machine.

Tip

Installing more than one protocol on a Windows machine very often results in browsing problems. Stick to TCP/IP.

DHCP and the Samba server

As a final tool in ensuring WINE full interoperability in a networked environment, this section discusses setting up the *Dynamic Host Control Protocol* (*DHCP*) under Samba. The assumption in the remainder of this section is that you have obtained DHCP server source files from ftp://ftp.isc.org/isc/dhcp, and that you have compiled and installed the dhcp daemon dhcpd. Assuming this to be the case, you need only implement a configuration file like that offered below.

dhcpd configuration files

dhcpd requires two configuration files:

- One that specifies the daemon's own settings
- One that contains the daemon's database of issued IP addresses

On most Intel Unix systems, the first of these files appears in the directory /etc, with a name such as dhcpd.conf. The second most frequently occurs as part of the file /etc/hosts.

A partial example of dhcpd.conf follows.

```
subnet 172.10.1.0 netmask 255.255.255.0 {
range 172.10.1.1 172.16.1.100;
        default-lease-time 72000;
```

```
max-lease-time 72000;
option subnet-mask 255.255.255.0;
option broadcast-address 172.16.1.255;
option routers 172.16.1.254;
option domain-name-servers 172.16.1.1, 172.16.1.2;
option domain-name "some_outfit.com";
option time-offset 39600;
option ip-forwarding off;
option netbios-name-servers 172.16.0.1;
option netbios-dd-server 172.16.0.1;
option netbios-node-type 8;
}
```

 Tip

As one commentator on the topic puts it, in order for dhcpd to work correctly with picky DHCP clients such as Windows 95, it must be able to send packets with an IP destination address of 255.255.255.255. Most versions of Linux, however, will by default substitute the local subnet broadcast address. As a result, a DHCP protocol violation occurs, which, while it may be ignored by many clients, will cause some, such as Windows 95, to fail to see certain categories of messages from the DHCP server. One can work around this problem under some Intel Unix versions by creating a route from the network interface address to 255.255.255.255. An example of a command that will accomplish this on most recent Linux distributions is

```
route add -host 255.255.255.255 dev eth0
```

Commercial Interoperability Tools

While a number of commercial interoperability tools exist, we will focus here on only one. Since Microsoft's strategic plans center on Windows 2000, whose kernel relies on the Windows NT rather than the Windows 9*x* model, and since, therefore, WINE will very likely have to interoperate more and more with NT-like APIs, this section presents overviews of several Windows NT–supported NFS Servers.

NFS servers on Windows NT

The ability to run an NFS server under Windows NT depends on a number of factors discussed in the remainder of this section.

The Windows 9x and the Windows NT APIs

While Windows 95 and Windows NT share a large part of the Win32 API, they implement it in significantly different ways in a number of areas. Table 5-4 summarizes these differences.

Table 5-4 *Windows 95 and Windows NT API Differences*

Feature	Handled Under Windows 95	Handled Under Windows NT
Network and file system device drivers	as virtual drivers	some APIs inherited from OS/2
	intended to be written in assembly language	other APIs modeled after VAX/VMS
		must be written in C or a
	adequate support in Developers' Kit	language which can call C
		like other Win32 APIs, not documented
		like other Win32 APIs, data structures and other details of source code change from release to release of NT

As a result of such idiosyncracies in the Windows NT API, only a few commercial NFS servers are available for Windows NT 4.0.

Windows NT resource sharing

The Intel Unix file administrative model includes

- User IDs
- Group IDs
- Access to files and directories based upon the distinction between owning, having group ownership of, or no ownership of, those files and directories
- A default set of read/write/execute rights assigned to every newly created file or directory

Windows NT, on the other hand, relies on

- User names
- Group names
- Default groups

to assign access rights under the FAT file system. Under NTFS, on the other hand, Windows NT offers access rights by directory or file that include

- List
- Read
- Add
- Add and read
- Change
- Full control

Therefore, if WINE is to share NT resources by means of NFS, the names of such resources must be of the form required under Intel Unix. Most current commercial NFS clients offer this ability. No server package does so. At best, such servers require an administrator to do such things as

- Manually create mappings between NT and Intel Unix user and group names
- Ensure that the Intel Unix and NT user names and password are the same for all those who intend to use NFS to bridge the OSes

Protocols needed by NFS

In order for you to share files through NFS, several protocols must run on the NFS server. These protocols include

- Portmapper, also called RPCBind in its newer versions
- mountd, the mount daemon
- nlockmgr, a lock manager
- NFS itself

All these protocols make calls to the portmapper, assumed to be on TCP port 111, in order to locate the TCP or UDP port on a remote machine where the other member protocols are running.

Specific commercial NFS servers for NT

The remainder of this section evaluates a number of such NFS servers according to the criteria just defined.

SuperNFS SuperNFS from Frontier Technologies has been reported as experiencing problems configuring exports and mappings.

Maestro This NFS server from Hummingbird

- Supports only Solaris
- Mounts NFS file systems from Solaris only if those file systems have been specified as read-only.

NFS server The NFS Server product of NetManage has been reported as

- Providing no means of specifying read-write or read-only access
- Incorrectly reporting directory sizes

InterDrive NFS server The InterDrive NFS server from FTP Software does not support read-only file systems.

Disk Share Disk Share from InterGraph supports

- NFS version 3
- File read and write packet requests and replies as large as 64KB

and was the only NFS server reported to operate without significant glitches.

Part III

Troubleshooting

Chapter 6

Troubleshooting Standalone WINE Implementations

XFree86

WINE's displays rely on the correct configuration of XFree86, its most common underlying windowing system. This section reviews that configuration.

Configuration tips

Assuming you're working with a recent release of Linux, configuring XFree86 to interact correctly with mouse, keyboard, monitor, and video card is an almost painless process. What follows is a list of points related to that configuration which will allow it to proceed as smoothly as possible.

- If you're using the setup program *XF86Setup*, be aware that it invokes a VGA16 server and tells it to start X Windows in a baseline 640 × 480 mode. Then XF86Setup runs an interactive configuration utility that covers five areas: mouse, keyboard, video adapter, monitor, and other server options.

- Versions of Red Hat Linux prior to 6.*x* use a similar but not identical X Windows configuration utility called *xf86config*. xf86config differs from XF86Setup in providing no X interface, and in not working with the VGA16 server.

- Most keyboards today fall into the category XF86Setup calls *Generic 102-key PC (intl)*. As a result, if you pick the default 101-key keyboard at this point in the setup, the numeric keypad on the extreme right of your keyboard may not work properly.

- If you're not sure of your monitor type, work your way through the listed choices from top to bottom. Selections early in the list indicate slower display speeds that are less demanding on video hardware.

- When you reach the *xvidtune* portion of XF86Setup, which allows you to fine-tune video performance, don't be alarmed by its warnings. The monitors to which those warnings pertain are older, fixed-frequency types. More modern monitors almost never can be damaged in the way these warnings suggest.

- xf86config sometimes assumes that the Linux device designation for a mouse is /dev/mouse. If your mouse doesn't work properly with this designation, you may need to link /dev/mouse to whatever entry in /dev your mouse is actually connected to.

 Tip

XFree86 configuration essentially selects an X server appropriate to your video card and sets up a configuration file, XF86Config, that the chosen server will read on startup to get specific parameters for your system.

Troubleshooting

Should your X Windows display

- Roll intermittently
- Have indistinct, fuzzy edges

the most likely cause is that monitor timing values, dot clocks, or video card chipset were incorrectly specified during setup. To correct such problems, review the Device section of XF86Config, and if need be bring erroneous entries into agreement with your hardware's documented requirements.

If verifying and correcting XF86Config doesn't correct display deficiencies, verify that you are using the X server appropriate to your equipment. Also ensure that there is a symbolic link from /usr/X11R6/bin/X to this appropriate server.

Should nothing else debug your X display, take these steps to produce further clues.

1. Use the command

   ```
   X > /tmp/x.out 2>&1
   ```

   This command

   - Redirects the output of the X server to a file in the temporary directory

   - Redirects any warning or error messages the X server generates to the same file

2. Let X run for a bit, then kill it with the keystroke combination Ctrl+C or Ctrl+Alt+Backspace.

3. Examine the contents of /tmp/x.out for clues.

Manual fine-tuning

XFree86 configurations cannot, out of the box, support monitors with resolutions higher than 1280 × 1024. Therefore, monitors that offer the highest resolutions, such as 1600 × 1200, must have their X configuration manually fine-tuned if they are to provide optimum performance. Should you need to do such fine-tuning, you can get an excellent guide at `http://metalab.unc.edu/LDP/HOWTO/XFree86-Video-Timings-HOWTO.html`.

Configuring for 16-bit color depth

Should you need to run advanced graphics applications, XFree86's default 8-bit depth, 256-color palette may not suffice. In some cases, such applications perform better with 16-bit color depth and its resulting 65,536-color palette.

On some systems, getting 16-bit color depth and the resulting several dozen thousand colors requires only the following:

- In the screen section of XF86Config, having the line

  ```
  DefaultColorDepth 16
  ```

- Starting X with the command

  ```
  startx - -bpp 16
  ```
- Or editing the system file .xserverrc to add the line

  ```
  exec X :0 -bpp 16
  ```

If you use xdm as your windowing manager, you may instead need to modify the file *Xservers*, most often found in the path /etc/X11/xdm/. Ordinarily this file contains only a single uncommented line similar to this.

```
0 local /usr/X11R6/bin/X
```

Edit this line to add the parameter

```
-bpp 16
```

so that the modified line then resembles the example below.

```
0 local /usr/X11R6/bin/X -bpp 16
```

Finally, in the screen section of XF86Config, make sure you have the line

```
DefaultColorDepth 16
```

When Programs Running Under WINE Hang

Should an application running under WINE hang, take these steps.

1. Open an xterm window.
2. Use this command to get the process-ID of the stalled application.

   ```
   ps -a | grep wine
   ```
3. Terminate the offending process with the following command. Be sure to substitute the actual process identification number for the generalized parameter pid shown below.

   ```
   kill pid
   ```

Then restart WINE in debug mode. From this point on, you must examine the debugger's output in order to try to determine

- The reason for the problem, most frequently found in the last call reported by the debugger, usually in a line like the following:

```
Call KERNEL.90: LSTRLEN(0227:0692 "text")
ret=01e7:2ce7 ds=0227
```

- From the source code for the offending function, any recommended traces

Then once again restart WINE with this generalized syntax, ensuring that the correct name is substituted for the placeholder *xyz* shown below.

```
./wine -debugmsg +xyz,+relay
```

Tip

Should X Windows not respond to your attempt to open an xterm window, switch to such a console window by pressing Ctrl+Alt+F1. Then log in and proceed with the steps described. Or, if you kill WINE with

```
kill -HUP pid
```

WINE will automatically restart in debug mode.

Tip

Because WINE itself multithreads, ps is likely to report multiple occurrences of the WINE process. You can kill all such occurrences with a single command by typing

```
killall wine
```

When Programs Running Under WINE Report Errors

Some programs report errors or warnings by means of what some members of the WINE Project call *nondescript message boxes*. Since the problems that give rise to such boxes usually occur immediately before the message box appears, use WINE's debugger in this way to target those problems.

1. Start WINE with this syntax:

```
./wine -debug -debugmsg +all
```

2. Set a break point for the debugger with this command:

```
break MessageBoxA
```

Tip

MessageBoxA is the routine commonly called by both Win16 and Win32 applications to create boxes such as those described here.

3. Proceed through the debugging with this command:

```
continue
```

With this sequence of commands, WINE will stop immediately before setting up the message box. At this point, you must again examine the debugger's output in order to try to determine any recommended traces.

Early Program Crashes

Use a special trick to help debug any applications running under WINE which crash at such an early point in their load phase that the WINE debugger can't keep up with them.

1. Issue this command, being sure to substitute the name of the offending application for the generic parameter program we've used:

```
./wine -debugmsg +relay program
```

2. Such a command line will produce a listing of the functions the program in question calls in its startup section. Next, use this command to enter the WINE debugger:

```
./wine -debug winfile.exe.
```

3. Once the debugger starts,

    a. set a breakpoint on any function that you determined the errant program calls in its startup section

    b. type **c** (for continue) to bypass the calls Winfile is sure to make to this function, until you reach the point at which the offending function is called by the crashing startup section

Tip

These commands will create a lot of output. Only about the first 200 such lines are of interest to WINE's developers, who ask that you post any such lines as a bug report to the USENET newsgroup `comp.emulators.ms-windows.wine`. Along with this bug report, be sure to include information about your environment, such as the version of Intel Unix and release number of its kernel under which you ran WINE, as well as the name and version of the program which evoked the errors.

Summarizing the WINE Debugger

Table 6-1 briefly describes commands available within the WINE debugger.

Table 6-1 *Common Debugging Commands*

Command	Purpose
info reg	Displays information about registers.
info stack	Displays hexadecimal values from the stack.
info local	Displays the contents of local variables.
list <*line number*>	Lists source code.
x 0x4269978	Examines the contents of a memory location. Formats available to x are
	x longword hexadecimal (32-bit integer)
	d longword decimal
	w word hexadecimal
	b byte
	c single character
	s null-terminated ASCII string
	i i386 instruction
	A number can be specified before the format to indicate a repeating group. For example, listing 10 instructions after a given address could be done with a command like this: `x /10i 0x000001cd`.
? or help	Displays help.
q	Quits the debugger.

Continued

Table 6-1 *Continued*

Command	Purpose
bt	Performs a backtrace. That is, shows a history of WINE calls. Addresses displayed are, however, return addresses, not calling addresses.
cont	Continues executing program until a breakpoint or error condition is encountered.
define	Equates a symbol to a value. Example: `define myproc 0x000001c6`.
disable	Turns off a specific breakpoint. To disable a breakpoint, you need to find the breakpoint number with the info command. For example, to disable a breakpoint you've determined to be listed as number 1, simply type `disable 1,`
enable	Reenables a previously disabled breakpoint.
break	Defines breakpoints.
<Enter> (i.e., the Enter key)	Repeats the command most recently executed.

Other Debugging Tools

Table 6-2 outlines other tools useful for debugging WINE.

Table 6-2 *Debugging Tools for WINE*

This Tool	Available From	Functions As
IDA	`ftp://ftp.uni-koeln.de/ pc/msdos/programming/ assembler/ida35bx.zip`	Disassembler to trace DOS and Windows calls such as those to interrupts.
Pedump	`http://oak.oakland.edu/ pub/simtelnet/win95/ prog/pedump.zip`	Dumps the imports and exports of a *PE* or *Portable Executable* DLL.
XRAY	`ftp://ftp.th-darmstadt. de/pub/machines/ms-dos/ SimTel/msdos/asmutil/ xray15.zip`	DOS disassembler to trace DOS calls such as those to interrupts. Of greatest value when used in combination with Windows disassemblers.

Chapter 7

Troubleshooting in Networked Environments

If WINE is to function properly when paired with an interoperability tool such as Samba, not only WINE itself but its partner may have to be debugged or have its performance optimized.

Testing, Debugging, and Fine-Tuning Samba

To ensure WINE a sound interconnectivity platform in Samba, there are a number of steps you can take.

Test smb.conf

If its configuration file smb.conf file contains errors, Samba will not even load. To test smb.conf before completing your Samba installation, use this command:

```
testparm smb.conf
```

This command will report any basic syntax or logical errors in the configuration file.

Test printing with smbclient

Should any Windows clients encounter trouble printing from applications running under WINE on a printer made available by a Samba server, you can test that server's printing configuration from the client itself. Follow these steps:

1. Connect to the server with a command like the following. Be sure to replace the generic parameter \\server\printer in this command with the correct network designation for the host and printer you're trying to reach.

   ```
   smbclient \\server\printer -P
   ```

2. Once connected, use the print command defined for the Samba server in question.

3. Should this print command fail, consult the smb.conf file for the server in question in order to debug printing configuration appropriately.

Debug CD-ROM mounts

Many versions of Linux auto-detect file types on CD-ROM drives and automatically do carriage return–line feed translation on these files. When done on applications being served to WINE by Samba, such translations can cause significant drive access and network transmission delays. Should your environment experience such delays, use a command like the following to mount your CD-ROM drive before identifying it to Samba. Be sure to substitute the device designation Linux expects for the CD-ROM drive for the generic parameter shown in this command.

```
mount /dev/somecd conv=binary
```

Tip

Jim Barry of the Samba Project has written an excellent conversion utility that takes carriage returns to line feeds and can be run completely in drag and drop fashion. Using this converter, you need only drag the file you need to convert onto the icon, which then converts the file. You can download this handy tool from ftp://samba.org/pub/samba/contributed/fix-crlf.zip.

Expedite user and password authentication

WINE and applications running under it must be readily available if Windows users are to be satisfied with the performance of their favorite programs in an Intel Unix environment. If you've ensured matches between user accounts on your WINE/Samba platform and its Windows clients, add this line to the [global] section of smb.conf:

```
security = user
```

Such an entry guarantees that

- Passwords are checked only when a user first connects
- Subsequent connections by that user to printers, disks, or any other resource will be processed much more quickly than they would otherwise have been had the entry not been present

Caution

Using this technique under Windows for Workgroups has a drawback. In such a case, a user can connect to a Samba server configured with security = user only by supplying the user name needed to log into Windows for Workgroups initially. No other user account, however well-duplicated on the Linux side, will suffice.

Expedite printer management

To ensure

- The ability to delete print jobs from the queue of a printer made available through a Samba server
- The ability to receive accounting information for such a printer

make sure that the following lines appear in smb.conf on the server:

- guest ok = no (in the [printer] section)
- security = user (in the [global] section)

Update TCP/IP stacks

Early Microsoft implementations of TCP/IP stacks had, in the words of members of the Samba Project, *lots of bugs*. Needless to say, such stacks might prove particularly problematic to someone working with both Samba and applications running under WINE.

At regular intervals, Microsoft has released upgrades to their 32-bit TCP/IP VxD (virtual) drivers. The latest release can be downloaded from the Microsoft ftp site `ftp.microsoft.com`; the file to pull down is */peropsys/windows/public/tcpip/wfwt32.exe*. The file *update.txt* that accompanies this executable describes the communications problems the download can help fix. Some of the individual files included in the download are

- WINSOCK.DLL
- TELNET.EXE
- WSOCK.386
- VNBT.386
- WSTCP.386
- TRACERT.EXE
- NETSTAT.EXE
- NBTSTAT.EXE.

Use nmbd as a WINS server

Allowing Samba clients to use a WINS server rather than their default practice of broadcasting to find shares can

- Greatly reduce network broadcast traffic
- Allow clients to find shares across routers

Configure Samba to act as a WINS server by adding the following line to the [globals] section of smb.conf.

```
wins support = yes
```

Then configure Windows for Workgroups, Windows 9x, or Windows NT clients to recognize nmbd on the Samba server as a WINS server with a line like the following in the [global] section of each client's smb.conf.

Be sure to substitute the correct IP address of the Samba/WINS server for the generic value used in this example.

```
wins server = 123.4.567.8
```

Caution

nmbd may not support all WINS operations your environment might request.

Debugging a Samba server

This section consists of a series of tests through which you can validate a Samba server and offers likely causes of the failure of any one of these tests. These tests should be carried out in the indicated order.

These tests assume

- A Samba server called my_srvr
- A Samba client called yur_client, running Windows 95 and a recent copy of the Microsoft TCP/IP stack
- An available share on the Samba server, called for_all
- That your /etc/resolv.conf file accurately points to appropriate name servers
- The setting `dns proxy = no` in the `[global]` section of your Samba server's smb.conf

You will, of course, have to adjust the syntax of the commands that make up these tests to reflect the configuration of your Samba server and clients.

Caution

Some of the commands used in these tests do not exist in early versions of Samba.

Test smb.conf

In the directory that houses smb.conf, run this command:

```
testparm smb.conf
```

If testparm reports any errors, you must debug your server's Samba configuration file.

Tip

Your smb.conf file may be located in /etc or in /usr/local/samba/lib.

Test server/client connectivity with ping

Run this command from your Samba client:

```
ping my_srvr
```

Run this command from your Samba server:

```
ping yur_client
```

Should either command not report successful communication, you're faced with having to reinstall TCP/IP.

Tip

At the client end, ping can be run only from the DOS command line.

Tip

ping can sometimes fail even when your TCP/IP installation is impeccable. If your Samba server is behind a firewall, that application's configuration may need to be relaxed.

Test the receipt of session requests

Run this command from your Samba server:

```
smbclient -L my_srvr
```

The command should produce a list of available shares.

Should the command fail, examine and if necessary correct any lines of the following forms in smb.conf.

```
hosts allow =
hosts deny =
```

```
valid users =
invalid users =
```

Should the command fail with the error

```
session request failed
```

the Samba server has refused the connection, and there are two steps you need to take:

1. Check smb.conf with testparm.

2. Ensure that the various directories where Samba wants to keep its log and lock files actually exist and have appropriate access permissions.

 Tip

The most common reasons for a session request to be refused involve one or more of the following sample smb.conf entries:

```
hosts deny = ALL
hosts allow = 123.45.678.09/24
bind interfaces only = Yes
```

In these sample lines, no provision has been made for session requests that translate to the loopback address 127.0.0.1. Solve this problem by changing these lines as indicated below.

```
hosts deny = ALL
hosts allow = 123.45.678.09/24 127
```

 Tip

Having something already running on port 139 when a Samba server expects to use that port for the smbd daemon can also cause this type of error. To determine if this might happen in your environment, check your Internet daemon configuration file inetd.conf before trying to start smbd as a daemon.

Test server IP address lookup

Run this command from your Samba server:

```
nmblookup -B my_srvr  SAMBA
```

The command should return the IP address of your Samba server. Should this fail, you can assume that your nmbd daemon has not been correctly installed. To correct this, check inetd.conf to ensure that nmbd runs from and listens at UDP port 137.

Test client IP address lookup

Run this command from your Samba server:

```
nmblookup -B yur_client '*'
```

The command should return the IP address of the Samba client. Should it fail, check

- The correctness of the configuration of the Samba client
- That the Samba client software has indeed been launched
- That you've supplied the correct machine name for the Samba client

Test broadcast address lookup

Run this command from your Samba server:

```
nmblookup -d 2 '*'
```

The purpose of this command is to connect to the nmbd daemon by means of a broadcast to the default broadcast address. A number of NetBIOS/TCPIP hosts on the network should respond, and you should see the following message from each of these several responding machines:

```
got a positive name query response
```

Should you not see such messages, nmblookup isn't correctly getting broadcast addresses through its automatic mechanism. In such cases you'll have to experiment with the interfaces option in the [global] section of smb.conf to configure your IP address, broadcast, and netmask correctly. For example, to configure two network interfaces with IP addresses 123.456.7.8 and 123.456.8.9, respectively, you could use this line:

```
interfaces = 123.456.7.8/24 23.456.8.9/24
```

Or, you could produce an equivalent result with this line:

```
interfaces = 123.456.7.8/255.255.255.0   123.456.7.9/255.255.255.0
```

Test user name/password configuration

Run this command from your Samba server:

```
smbclient \\my_srvr\for_all
```

When the command runs, you should see a prompt for a password. In response, supply the password of the account you used to log into Intel Unix on the machine housing your Samba server.

Having supplied the password, the next thing you see should be the Samba prompt

```
smb>
```

Should you instead receive the error

```
bad password
```

the likely causes include:

- Your Intel Unix platform runs shadow passwords or another similar password system, but you neglected to compile support for them into smbd
- You have a mixed-case password but failed to initialize the smb.conf parameter *password level* at a high enough level
- You enabled password encryption but didn't create an encrypted SMB password file
- You incorrectly configured the smb.conf *valid users* parameter
- You incorrectly configured the smb.conf *path* parameter

After homing in on and correcting the source of the error, carry out one last test to verify your changes. Compare the amount of free disk space reported by Samba's *dir* command with that reported by the operating system. If they match, you've got full connectivity to the Samba server.

Test NetBIOS name resolution

From a DOS prompt on the Samba client, run this command:

```
net view \\my_srvr
```

In response, you should get a list of available shares on your server. If instead you see the error messages

```
network name not found
```

you've learned that NetBIOS name resolution has failed. Problems with nmbd's configuration usually cause this error. To correct such problems, try the following.

- Verify nmbd's configuration
- Ensure that the IP address of my_srvr appears in the WINS server list of the client's Advanced TCP/IP setup
- Enable DNS-based Windows name resolution with the same client dialog
- Add my_srvr to the client's *lmhosts* file

Test client configuration

Run this command:

```
net use x: \\my_srvr\tmp
```

You should see a prompt for a password, and the message

```
command completed successfully
```

Should these not appear,

- You may have incorrectly installed the Samba client software
- You may have incorrectly configured the client's smb.conf

To correct the problem, check that file, particularly the parameter *hosts allow*.

Net use may also fail because the Samba server can't match the user name you've supplied with one to which it can connect users. You can add the following line to the [tmp] section of smb.conf on the server to solve this problem. Be sure to substitute the user name appropriate to the password you just supplied for the generic parameter shown below.

```
user = some_usr
```

Test browsing

From Windows Explorer or File Manager, try to browse the Samba server. That server should appear in the browse list of your workgroup. Double-click on the name of the server; you should then see a list of shares. Ordinarily, failures of this test occur

- Under Windows NT
- Because NT refuses to browse a server that doesn't use encrypted passwords
- Because NT refuses to browse a server that is in user level security mode

Two alternative solutions exist.

- Set two parameters in your Samba server's smb.conf file as follows:

    ```
    security = server
    password server = Windows_NT_Machine
    ```
- Enable encrypted passwords on your Samba server after compiling in support for them.

Configuring for speed

Optimizing WINE's performance in a heterogeneous environment can include optimizing Samba's performance. The balance of this section contains tips for doing the latter. Each of these tips pertains to a specific parameter in smb.conf.

oplocks

Since managers rarely need to change the default value of this parameter, they can actually remove it from smb.conf. Doing so reduces processing time for the configuration file and can significantly improve Samba server performance.

getwd cache

Enabling this tuning option enables a caching algorithm used to reduce time used in getwd() calls and can therefore significantly improve overall performance. Set getwd cache to *yes*.

debug level

Through its integer values, this parameter specifies the extent to which Samba will log errors and problems. While you can set it to 0 to completely disable logging, setting debug level to 1 provides some debugging insights without overworking the Samba server.

null passwords

Slow processing of logins, and slow browsing, can be improved by removing the following line from the Samba server's smb.conf:

```
null passwords = yes
```

read raw

Since its default is *yes*, removing this line from smb.conf reduces processing time for the configuration file.

write raw

Like read raw, the default value for this parameter is *yes*. As a result, removing this line from smb.conf reduces processing time for the configuration file.

Appendix A

Fine-Tuning WINE

This summary discusses techniques for improving the performance of WINE and applications running under it by improving overall system performance.

Memory and CPU

Linux uses a demand-paged virtual memory system. Linux processes have a 4GB virtual memory space. As needed, this space acts as the go-between for pages transferred between disk and physical memory.

When physical memory pages are unavailable, the kernel swaps older pages back to disk. Therein lies the central problem of memory management. Drives, because they are mechanical devices, read and write at rates several orders of magnitude slower than those that pertain to accessing physical memory. Therefore, if the total memory pages required significantly exceed the physical memory available, the kernel starts spending more time swapping pages than executing code. The system slows down woefully and can even come to a standstill.

The remainder of this section examines detecting and correcting such intertwined memory/CPU performance problems.

Commands for Fine-tuning Memory and CPU

Fine-tuning memory or processor usage under Intel Unix relies on commands including:

- cron, through which diagnostics can be scheduled to run at specific intervals
- free, which reports the amount of free swap space
- ps, which gives varying amounts of detail on process status
- top, which displays real-time CPU statistics
- vmstat, which tracks virtual, rather than physical, memory
- ls in combination with sort

Make efficient use of these commands by

1. using ps to try to home in on processes that run inordinately slowly.

2. running both free and vmstat immediately before and after starting an application under WINE.

3. running both free and vmstat at regular intervals, possibly by means of a script submitted to the cron scheduling command.

 Tip

Interpreting the output of these commands may be difficult or misleading. Linux uses much of its available memory for file cache buffers. What's more, large percentages of both shared libraries and memory allocated to forked processes is shared. Finally, the Linux memory manager uses several techniques to minimize the degree to which the system draws upon physical memory. As a result, getting an accurate reading of actual memory usage may take time.

Nonetheless, try to isolate memory usage per program to as high a degree as possible. Then, for any programs that seem unusually memory-voracious, try to obtain any update available for it, or for any of the libraries it uses. Also, consider getting a newer version of your OS kernel.

The remainder of this section sets out basic syntax for each of these commands.

cron

Understanding cron means understanding its scheduling file *crontab*, usually found in the directory /etc.

The following is an example of a line from /etc/crontab:

`0 13 * * 1-6 /usr/leila/check_mem`

Tables A-1 and A-2 explain the space-delimited fields in a crontab entry, and in our example entry respectively.

Table A-1 *Understanding crontab Entries*

Field	Significance to cron
first	The minute at which you wish to schedule a job, specified as an integer in the range 0 through 59.
second	The hour at which you wish to schedule a job, specified as an integer in the range 0 through 23, with 0 representing midnight.
third	The date of the month at which you wish to schedule a job, specified as an integer in the range 1 through 31.
fourth	The month at which you wish to schedule a job, specified as an integer in the range 1 through 12.
fifth	The day of the week at which you wish to schedule a job, specified as an integer in the range 0 through 6, with 0 representing Sunday.
sixth	The command you want to run at the indicated interval.

Table A-2 *Understanding a Sample crontab Entry*

Field	Significance to cron
0	Run the command indicated in the final field on the hour, that is, at the zero-th minute of every hour.
13	Run the command indicated in the final field at the thirteenth hour, that is, at 1:00 PM.
* 31.	Run the command indicated in the final field on every date of the month from 1 through
*	Run the command indicated in the final field on every month from 1 through 12.
1-6	Run the command indicated in the final field every Sunday through Friday.
/usr/leila/ check_mem	The full path name of the script that checks memory usage, and that cron will schedule as you've indicated.

Tip

The crontab file contains only text and can therefore be edited with any text editor. Because cron runs as a daemon in the background, there's no other way to invoke it than to feed it tasks to run from crontab.

free

Simply typing

```
free
```

causes Intel Unix to report:

- Free swap space
- Free RAM
- Shared memory
- Buffered memory

A partial sample of the output of free appears below.

```
Total   used   free   shared   buffers
Mem
 7096   5216   1880   2328     2800
Swap
19464      0  19464
```

free reports in kilobytes. Total memory is that which is available after the kernel has been loaded. used indicates memory that is used for processes or disk buffering. Only memory not used for either of these purposes is displayed in the "free" column. Memory reported as shared indicates how much memory is common to more than one process, while that which is used for disk buffering shows up in the "buffers" column.

Tip

The latter category is particularly important to WINE. WINE must share memory with any other processes being run under the shell in which WINE was started.

ps

ps, short for *process status*, identifies processes by their *PID* or *process ID number*. Table A-3 summarizes ps.

Table A-3 *Commonly Used ps Parameters*

Parameter	Effect on ps
-a	gives information on all processes, whether started by the system or a user
-e	gives information on all processes, started from any terminal
-l	gives a long – that is, a detailed – listing of process information
-u username	gives a listing of processes started by the user you specify by user name

The output of *ps -l* is indeed extensive, including:

- Address in memory of the process
- Number of blocks of memory the process uses
- Cumulative time the process has been running
- Name of the command represented by the PID parameter
- Percentage of CPU used by the process
- Priority at which the process executes, expressed as an integer; note that the lower the priority number, the higher the process's priority
- Process ID number
- Process ID number of the current task's parent process
- Process status, expressed as a single letter such as *S (sleeping)*, *W (waiting)*, *T (terminated)*, and *R (running)*
- Special indicators associated with the process, presented as octal numbers
- Terminal from which the process was started
- User ID of the user who started the process

The following illustrates a simple use of ps:

```
ps -e
```

Table A-4 describes possible output of such a command.

Table A-4 *Understanding ps*

Output				Significance
PID	TTY	TIME	COMMAND	headers for ps output
0	?	4:21	swapper	that the swapper, which shuttles commands and data in and out of memory and whose process ID is 0, was not started from a specific station, but has been running for four minutes and 21 seconds
1	?	0:01	init	that the system's shell initialization routine init, whose process ID is 1, was not started from any specific station, but has been running for one second
13	t0	0:07	sh	that the current shell, indicated by sh and whose process ID is 13, was started from the station /dev/t0, and has been running for seven seconds

To track use of both the operating system and WINE by a specific user, try a command like the following. Of course, be sure to substitute the user name of the individual whose activities on the system you wish to track for the hypothetical user name in this example.

```
ps -u resource_hog
```

To track processes started from a specific station during its current session, use a command like the following. Remember to substitute an actual station designation for the generic indicator in this sample command.

```
ps -t t0
```

top

The command top is impressive, giving as it does a real-time snapshot of CPU activity as outlined in Table A-5.

Table A-5 *Understanding top*

Parameter	Significance
−s *some integer*	sets top's display to refresh in the number of seconds you specify
−d	tells top to present only the specified number of displays, and then to quit
−u	tells top to include in its display user ID numbers rather than user names
−n	tells top to show per screen only the number of processes you specify

Use a command like the following to start the light show that top produces.

```
top -s 4
```

Among the output top offers are

- averages of loads on the CPU over the most recent several time intervals
- number of processes currently in the CPU
- number of processes in any of several conditions such as sleeping, waiting, running, starting, or stopped
- percentage of its time that the CPU has spent, since top's last report, in any of several conditions such as idle and interrupt; on multiprocessor systems, supplied per CPU

Tip

You must use the keystroke sequence Ctrl+C to terminate top and return to the system prompt if you haven't supplied the -d option.

vmstat

vmstat reports virtual memory, process, and total CPU statistics for a specified time interval. The first line of its output covers all time since a reboot, and each subsequent report is for the most recent increment you've specified at the command line. The following sample illustrates using vmstat.

```
vmstat 3
```

Sample output from this command appears as follows.

```
Virtual Memory Statistics: (pagesize = 8192)

procs    memory            pages                         intr         cpu
r  w  u  act  free wire  fault cow zero react pin pout    in  sy  cs  us sy  id
2 66 25  6417 3497 1570  155K 38K  50K    0  46K    0     4 290 165   0  2  98
4 65 24  6421 3493 1570  120    9  81     0   8     0   585 865 335  37 16  48
2 66 25  6421 3493 1570  69     0  69     0   0     0   570 968 368   8 22  69
4 65 24  6421 3493 1570  69     0  69     0   0     0   554 768 370   2 14  84
4 65 24  6421 3493 1570  69     0  69     0   0     0   865  1K 404   4 20  76
              [1]                                      [2]     [3]        [4]
```

Tip

Integer values in the range 2 to 5 make reasonable parameters for vmstat. Because CPUs operate faster than the other system components vmstat checks, it is not usually the source of performance bottlenecks. Rather, those more frequently arise from the memory or I/O subsystems.

Among the most important of vmstat's output fields are

- memory, including the number of pages on the active list
- number of pages that have been *paged out* (*pout*)
- number of pages free (free)
- number of pages active (act)
- number of pages wired (wire)
- interrupt information (intr), including the number of nonclock device interrupts per second (in), the number of system calls called per second (sy), and the number of task and thread context switches per second (cs).
- CPU usage information (cpu), including the percentage of user time for normal and priority processes (us), the percentage of system time (sy), and the percentage of idle time (id). Be aware that user time includes the time the CPU spent executing library routines.

When attempting to diagnose bottlenecks that affect WINE, keep these rules of thumb in mind:

- Use vmstat both when demands on the system drop and when they increase, in order to have some basis for understanding both these situations.

- Remember that the output of vmstat will be affected by atypical system events or by temporary increases in the demand for system resources.

- Check the size of the free page list; compare the number of free pages with those of active pages and wired pages. The sum of the sizes of your free, active, and wired pages should be close to the amount of physical memory in your system. What's more, while the value for free should be small, if it is consistently less than 128 pages and accompanied by excessive paging and swapping, you may have a physical memory problem.

- The number of pageouts can also reflect the lack of sufficient RAM. Should pout be consistently high, you may have insufficient memory or swap space, or your swap space may be configured inefficiently.

Every system administrator should seek to keep a CPU as productive as possible. Idle CPU cycles occur when no runnable processes exist or when the CPU is waiting to complete an I/O or memory request. vmstat can help diagnose such problems as well. Table A-6 explains vmstat's CPU-related output.

Table A-6 *Understanding CPU Statistics from vmstat*

Output	Significance
High user time combined with low idle time	Applications consume most of the CPU's efforts.
High system time combined with low idle time	Something in the application load stimulates the system with high overhead operations. Such operations could consist of high system call frequencies, high interrupt rates, large numbers of small I/O transfers, or large numbers of interprocess communication network transfers.
	May also indicate failing hardware.

Continued

Table A-6 *Continued*

Output	Significance
Very high system time regardless of other parameters	A condition known as thrashing, in which memory available to the virtual memory subsystem has gotten so low that the system is spending all its time paging and swapping in an attempt to regain memory. A system that spends more than 50 percent of its time in system mode and idle mode may be doing a lot of paging and swapping I/O, and therefore may have a virtual memory performance, that is, a thrashing problem.
High idle time coupled with poor response time, even under typical loads	Hardware may have reached its capacity; one or more kernel data structures may be overworked; hardware or kernel resource problems in areas such disk I/O may exist.
Very low idle time coupled with adequate performance	Your system uses its CPU efficiently.

Tip

Like top, free, and other system-monitoring commands, vmstat itself uses large amounts of OS resources. So don't watch its display for too long.

ls

Examine some of your larger executables to see if they were built with the appropriate compiler and linker options. To identify the largest programs, use a command like the following. Remember to choose an output file name more mnemonic than our sample parameter *biggies*.

```
ls -sl /bin /usr/bin /usr/local/bin | sort -n > biggies
```

This command searches the directories most likely to house huge executables, including that in which WINE resides. Such a command finds only the largest files in those paths, making it a good indicator of the memory requirements of the corresponding programs.

Tip

We've excluded the path /usr/bin/X11 from the example just given because, despite its very large size, WINE must have the full X Window complement of executables.

Recompiling the Kernel to Optimize Memory Usage

Unlike the memory pages used by processes, Intel Unix never swaps out kernel pages. Therefore, if you can reduce the size of the kernel, you can free up memory that can be used by WINE and applications running under it.

Recompile the kernel with only the options and device drivers absolutely needed. Kernels shipped with Linux distributions sometimes have every possible driver and file system compiled in so that any system can boot from it. If, however, your system has no CD-ROM or SCSI devices, you can save appreciable amounts of memory by removing drivers for such devices from the kernel.

Tip

Should your system need certain drivers only occasionally, consider building several kernels and setting up LILO to let you choose an alternate kernel when booting.

Tip

Make sure you run the most recent kernel possible. Newer kernels, in addition to being more stable, also manage memory more effectively.

Changing the Environment to Optimize Memory Usage

Under most versions of Intel Unix, one finds the GNU bash shell as the default command interpreter. bash, while feature-rich, is also quite large. Memory can be saved by substituting a smaller shell such as the *Korn shell* or *ksh* by means of editing the value associated with the system environment variable SHELL.

Disks

Disk input and output, and therefore the performance of applications running under WINE, can be improved by techniques that in turn rely on the command df.

df

df or disk free reports free disk blocks and free inodes available for file systems. If you specify no argument to df, it displays free space on all mounted file systems.

Some of df's results may seem odd. For example, path names supplied as arguments to df cause it to reports not on those paths, but on the file systems containing the paths.

Cause Intel Unix to report and categorize free disk space across an entire machine with this simple command:

```
df
```

Invoked in a slightly fuller form, df can report on specific file systems, producing output like that in the following example.

```
df /home
Filesystem   1k-blocks   Used    Available   Use%
Mounted on
/home        12345       97827   86544       51%
/dev/hda4
```

Load Balancing Based Upon df's Output

Once you identify burdened file systems, you can optimize the load upon them. Such load balancing follows two general techniques:

- Dividing a drive into several partitions, for example, to avoid having the root partition filled by user data. This technique has the disadvantage of partitions filling at significantly varying rates.
- Moving files from one partition or file system to another. Using symbolic links, you may be able to do this without affecting applications.

Choosing an appropriate size for your swap partition can also free disk space for applications like those running under WINE. But be careful in using this technique. Optimum swap partition size is a tradeoff between having adequate swap space and losing valuable file system space. Repartition to reduce swap space only if the free command reveals significant amounts of unused swap. Another alternative is to reduce the size of your swap partition but add a separate swap file on those occasions when extra swap is needed.

If your drives' file systems are load-balanced and disk space is still a problem, you may have to rely on the techniques described in the remainder of this section.

Finding Too-Large Files

Some students of disk use optimization subscribe to the 80/20 principle, which in effect states that 80 percent of a system's disk space is consumed by 20 percent of its files. Use the find command to locate all files on a system that are larger than a predetermined amount. For instance, you could try a command like this:

```
find / -size+1000000c —ls > listofbiggies
```

This command tells find to

- search the entire file system, starting at the root directory, for files larger than 1 million characters
- display listings in the style of the ls command for each such file found
- send final output to the named file

Removing Files

Before beginning to remove oversized files, remember these points:

- Back up what you're about to delete, just in case you need it again.
- Make sure you have a boot floppy to allow your machine to boot should you accidentally remove something vital, such as /vmlinuz.
- Rely on your distribution's package handling tools whenever possible to avoid removing distribution-installed files incorrectly.

The following list includes many candidates for removal without injury or loss of functionality. But be sure to have a good handle on your own system's needs before sending any of these to the big bit bucket in the sky.

- networking tools such as uucp newsreaders
- language tools such as lisp, smalltalk, TeX, and LaTeX
- source code, of particular importance to any who have custom-compiled WINE and are satisfied with its nature
- nroff source for man pages usually housed under /usr/man/, retaining only the compressed, formatted pages

X Window font files require a lot of disk space. Compress .pcf font files to buy back some of this storage. Be sure to run mkfontdir command after any such compression.

Truncating Files

Certain files grow without limit and should be periodically purged. Under many Intel Unix implementations, these files include:

- /etc/wtmp
- /etc/ftmp
- /var/log/notice

Truncate these files to zero length with a command like this:

```
cp /dev/null /var/log/notice
```

Truncate rather than delete files so that they will still be available to programs that use them but that may not re-create them.

Manipulating File Statuses to Optimize WINE

Two commands that manipulate a file's administrative information may also be useful in improving the performance of applications running under WINE.

touch

touch changes administrative information such as access and modification times and dates for the files whose names you give it as arguments. Table A-7 summarizes touch.

Table A-7 *Understanding touch*

Argument	Significance
-a	tells touch to alter only access time
-m *some date*	tells touch to alter only modification date. The date parameter must be supplied in the format *mmddhhnnyy*, for *month*/*day*/*hour*/*minute*/*year*
-c	tells touch to forgo creating a file for a name it doesn't recognize

Use touch like this:

```
touch -a 991212 file_of_stuf
```

This syntax assumes

- that December 13, 1999, is the current date
- that after the command runs, the file file_of_stuf will be shown by the ls command to have been accessed last on December 12, 1999

Unix and Linux administrators use touch for such things as

- ensuring that files will be recognized by jobs like date-dependant backups
- ensuring that files will be safe from jobs like date-driven automated deletions

It's in these sorts of situations that touch might be of value to the WINE administrator as well.

Managing User Accounts to Optimize WINE

Incorrectly or inefficiently configured user and group accounts and profiles may contribute to WINE, or the applications run under it, misbehaving. This section sets out some commands useful to monitoring and correcting user and group configuration.

chmod

Should a user not have file access permissions adequate to accomplishing what he or she needs to do with applications running under WINE, the fault may be seen to be with those applications, rather than with the poorly defined permissions. The chmod command can be used to adjust such permissions.

Either of two techniques can be used to change file access permissions with chmod. The first uses abbreviations of the permission to be enabled or disabled, as well as an indication of the user to whom the changes will apply. The second method supplies a three-octal-digit code, each of which digits represents file access permissions for

- a file's owner
- members of the owner's user group
- all other users on the system, respectively

Changing Permissions with Abbreviations

Use a command like the following to change file access permissions by means of mnemonic abbreviations.

```
chmod -w /usr/local/bin/wine
```

Such a command would prevent users' inadvertently modifying the WINE executable, by removing their ability to write to it.

Other operators with which chmod can work when used in this manner are:

- +: to add a permission to existing permissions for the file or directory in question
- =: to set, explicitly, all permissions for the file or directory in question to those specified after the equals sign

This form of chmod also understands the following parameters:

- u, which assigns access change to the file's owner

- g, which assigns access changes to members of the owner's group
- o, which assigns access changes to any other user, that is, to the world

Changing Permissions with Octal Codes

Another means of changing file access permissions involves supplying a three-digit number, each of whose digits represents a single set of permissions. For instance, the number 777 indicates that each of the three categories of users has every possible permission. The following sample command illustrates this technique, as does Table A-8:

```
chmod 711 /usr/local/bin/wine
```

Table A-8 *chmod's Octal Codes*

Octal Digit	Significance
7	read, write, and execute
6	read and write, but not execute
5	read and execute, but not write
4	read only
3	write and execute, but not read
2	write only
1	execute only
0	no permissions

In chmod's three-octal-digit codes, position is as significant as value. Those positions' applications can be outlined as follows:

- first digit: owner of file
- second digit: members of owner's group
- third digit: everyone else

TIP

An important security feature of Linux, called "immutable files," enhances system security by setting a file's mode to 000, thereby preventing any access whatsoever, until and unless the superuser modifies the mode to allow access.

Each of the octal digits that make up a number-based permission code breaks down into three binary digits. Each of these, in turn, represents the presence or absence of a particular access permission. For those of you not in the habit of mental octal-to-binary conversions, we offer a cheat sheet in Table A-9.

Table A-9 *Easy Octal to Binary Translation*

Octal Digit	Translates to
7	binary 111. Each of these binary digits grants the access permission corresponding to the position the digit occupies.
6	binary 110. Therefore grants read and write, but not execute, permission.
5	binary 101. Therefore grants read and execute, but not write, permission.
4	binary 100. Therefore grants only read permission.
3	binary 011. Grants write and execute but not read permissions. As such, might make a file completely inaccessible for such tasks as copying and renaming. Therefore almost universally avoided in most file access permissions, but possibly of use in protecting WINE.
2	binary 010. Grants only write permission.
1	binary 001. Grants only read permission.
0	binary 000. Therefore denies any access whatsoever to any users to whom it's applied. Very useful for keeping tinkerers from harming WINE, but don't use it in your own permissions.

chgrp

Of the same family as chmod and another similar command, chown, chgrp gives a file a new group affiliation.

Use a command like the following to change the group ID of a file or directory. Be sure to substitute parameters that make sense on your system, and that will positively rather than negatively affect your ability to access WINE.

```
chgrp techies /usr/local/wine
```

Such a command would assign group affiliation of the WINE executable to the user group *techies*, presumably made up of individuals skilled in this maintenance.

chown

Owners of files ordinarily have extensive control over those files. Therefore, it would probably be unwise on most systems to assign ownership of critical files to another user. However, it might be possible to expedite access to data files required by users running applications under WINE, with judicious use of the command chown. Use a command like this:

```
chown trusted_guy important_data
```

If

- your system recognizes trusted_guy as a legitimate user name
- important_data is a file you own, in the current directory

this command will make trusted_guy the new owner of important_data.

who

Should you suspect someone of lingering too long over his or her WINE, and depending on your particular Intel Unix implementation, the command who can supply such diverse information regarding logged-in users as:

- Time elapsed since the user's session became active
- Process ID of the user's shell
- The user's name

Such information can in turn be used to truncate or even terminate unnecessary user sessions.

To learn which users are currently connected to your Linux box, type this command:

```
who
```

Or you can use the following command to determine the length of time individual users have been logged in.

```
who -u
```

who -u doesn't do the math for you, but rather reports time of login. You're on your own from there.

Useful Utilities

This section briefly describes utilities available to Intel Unix for managing the resources discussed in this summary.

Autonice

Autonice, a simple Perl script, regularly surveys any CPU-hungry processes on a system. If any process uses more than a predefined amount of CPU time, the process is reniced — that is, its priority is lowered, and e-mail notifying the user who initiated the process is sent. Autonice has been successfully tested on Red Hat 4.*x* and higher and should run on any system using a crontab file and the /proc file system and having Perl installed.

- Version: Stable 1.0
- Size: 20.0 KB (20,480 bytes)
- License: Freely distributable
- Revision Date: June 27, 1999
- Home Page: http://www.nbi.dk/~kenand/autonice/autonice.html

Clobberd

Designed for ISPs but useful for general system monitoring, Clobberd tracks users and can limit their total logged-in time, logged-in time per day, CPU use, or memory use. Inversely, users can be designated exempt from such limitations.

- Version: Stable 4.10
- Size: 70.6 KB (72,248 bytes)
- License: GPL
- Revision Date: July 7, 1999
- Home Page: http://metalab.unc.edu/pub/Linux/system/admin/idle/
- Binary: RPM

Appendix B

Application Performance Summary

This summary examines

- the standards against which the WINE Project insists its product be tested
- significant excerpts from the results of such tests

Ratings Standards

The WINE Project asks that the behavior of applications run under WINE be rated according to the scale outlined in Table B-1, which, they state, "is pessimistic by design."

Table B-1 *WINE Application Ratings*

Rating	Means
0	Totally nonfunctional. Crashes on load
1	Loads without crashing. Good enough for a screenshot
2	Partial functionality. Good enough for a carefully scripted demo
3	Sufficient functionality for noncritical work. Occasional crashes okay, as are weird setup problems, required patches, or missing major functionality. Alpha quality
4	Substantially correct. Good enough for general use, with possible caveats
5	Perfect. No flaws under any mode

We've summarized the steps the WINE Project recommends for rating the performance of applications running under WINE.

1. Don't exaggerate how well things work. Doing so only creates expectations that can't be met, and doesn't do anybody any good in the long run.

2. First, figure out the name of the app, the vendor, and the product version number.

3. Try to start the application under WINE. If it loads without crashing, and displays more or less what it would under some version of Windows, then the app deserves a 1. Otherwise, it gets a zero.

4. Try doing a few things with it. If you can find several useful operations that can be correctly performed with the app, such that you would be willing to stand in front of a large group of people, saying "This app works nearly perfectly on WINE" and doing those operations, give it a 2. Otherwise, it's a 1.

5. If you don't normally use the app, stop here. Higher ratings should be given only for app performance under actual use.

6. At some time when there is something you need to do with the app, try doing it under WINE. If you can get the job done without putting your fist through the screen, the application deserves a 3. Note that this is not "Someone could do useful work with this app under WINE but I have used this app under WINE for useful work, not just fooling around."

7. If you use an app under WINE for months, its behavior is robust under a variety of uses, its performance is adequate, these characteristics are stable as WINE changes from release to release, and it works for a lot of people with varying setups under various OSes, then it deserves a 4.

8. Don't give 5's.

The Project further requests that anyone volunteering to test application performance under WINE report the following, along with ratings, to the WINE Project:

- what type of use best describes the application (the category)
- the Windows platform the application is intended for (the type)

- person, organization, or company that produced the application (the vendor)
- vendor URL
- full product name
- complete version number of the application
- names and versions of any native DLLs from any version of Microsoft Windows used during the tests
- platform WINE was run under, including version
- release date of the WINE version tested

Performance Summary

We present our summaries of application performance under WINE in several categories, the first being type/operating system, itself made up of:

- DOS
- Win16
- Win32
- Win32s
- Win NT

Within each of these groups, we present:

- A/V
- graphics
- hardware
- network
- office
- programming
- server

Note that, should any of these functional categories be missing in these summaries, no applications in that category were tested for the OS in question.

We complete the application performance summary with five categories:

- Miscellaneous applications — that is, those that do not fit readily into any of the foregoing groups

- Applications rated 5
- Applications rated 4
- Applications rated 3
- Office applications rated at least 3

Note that in each of the summaries below, we have

- excluded multiple test results — that is, the results of testing the same version of one product
- presented instead the mean value of the results of such multiple tests
- excluded test results for applications we considered to be too obscure
- included tests of different versions of the same product
- allowed results pertaining to a single product/version to appear in more than one functional category (e.g., a single application being shown in the results for A/V and graphics) where the WINE database actually did so

Before beginning the presentation of specific test results, however, we offer Table B-2, an overview of results in several of the foregoing categories.

Table B-2 *WINE Performance Statistics*

Category	Average Rating	Number in Category Rated 5	Number in Category Rated 4
DOS	2.7	17	35
Win16	2.7	35	105
Win32	2.2	100	281
Win32s	2.3	19	46
Windows NT	1.5	4	5

These statistics may, of course, no longer be exact, since they were compiled at the time this book was being prepared. We gathered them from the database of test results that the WINE Project maintains at www.winehq.com/Apps, which, at that time, contained nearly 2,000 reported results. Note also that the ratings that underlie these statistics are somewhat subjective.

Win16 Applications

This section summarizes the performance of 16-bit applications under WINE.

A/V

Vendor	Product	Version	Rating
Adobe	Acrobat Reader	2.1	3
Microsoft	Media Player		2
Microsoft	Encarta	95	3
Sirius	Movie CD		1
Thayer Birding Software	Birds of North America	2	0

Graphics

Vendor	Product	Version	Rating	
Alchemy Mindworks	GIF Construction Set	1.0Q	3	
Artec/Ultima	AS6E Scanner Driver	4		Autodesk
Autosketch	2	2		Cerious Software
ThumbsPlus	2.0a	5		Cognitive Technology
cuneiform	3.0	4		Corel
CorelDraw	3	2		GeoClock
GeoClock		2		Inovative Data Design
Windraft	1.2	5		Jasc
Media Center	2.02	4		Peanut Software
WinFeed fractal exploration program	August 99	3		Sky Scan
Digidome	2.0	3		SuperKey
SuperMap	USA	3		WNI Oceanroutes (UK) Ltd.
Saturn Weather Graphics System	1.03	2		WNI
Quark	Xpress	3.32	4	
Quark	Xpress	3.12	5	

Hardware

Vendor	Product	Version	Rating
Beige Bag Software	B2Logic	3	4
IBM	IBM Home Director		4
Microchip	MPASM for Windows	2.20	4
National Instruments	LabVIEW	4.1	4
SL/Waber	Electronic Bookmark for UPStart UPS Units	1.2	5

Network

Vendor	Product	Version	Rating
3Com	Quick Config Manager	4.01	2
AOL	AOL	3.0 (16-bit)	3
AOL	AOL	4	2
American Cybernetics	Multi-edit	7.11c1	3
Appgen	PowerWindows Client	4.1	3
CuteFTP	CuteFTP	2.0 (16-bit)	3
Excite	Excite PAL	1.11ex (16-bit)	4
Forte	Agent 16	1.5	2
Ipswitch Inc.	WS_FTP Client	4.60	5
Ipswitch Inc.	WS_FTP Limited Edition	3.10	5
Juno Email	Juno Mail	n/a	2
MIRC	mIRC	5.5	0
Microsoft	Windows Terminal Server Client	4.0	4
Microsoft	Exchange Client	5.0 (16-bit)	3
Microsoft	Internet Explorer	5	4
Netscape	Navigator Gold	3.0	5
Netscape Communications	Mozilla	Beta 0.93 (circa 1994)	4
Novell	Web Manager		1
Novell	GroupWise	5.2	3
ORL	VNC Viewer		0
Opera Software	Opera	3.60 (16-bit)	2

Vendor	Product	Version	Rating
Pegasus Mail	Pegasus Mail	3.01d	3
Qualcomm	Eudora Light	1.5.2	4
Softarc	First Class Client	3.1	5
	Teleport pro	1.29 (Build 772)	4
W.L. Ken	News Xpress	1.0b4-p	3

Office

Vendor	Product	Version	Rating
JASC	Paint Shop Pro	3.11	5
Adept Computer Solutions	Street Maps USA	6.00.11	3
Adobe	FrameMaker	5.4	0
Berlitz Publishing Company Ltd.	Berlitz Interpreter	2	3
CAS Software	GmbH Shell Auto Atlas	1.0	2
Corel	WordPerfect	8	0
Corel	Sidekick	2.0	0
DeScribe Corp.	DeScribe Word Processor	5.0/Windows 16	3
Digital	TEAMLINK for Windows	3.0-001	0
Inituit	Quicken	1.0	1
Intuit	Quicken	3	4
Intuit	Quicken	98	4
Intuit	Quicken	6	3
Kindred Konnections	Kindred Konnections	1.2	2
Kiplinger	Taxcut	1998 tax year	0
Lotus	1-2-3	Release 5	3
Lotus	Improv	2.0	3
Lotus	cc:Mail	2.2	1
Lotus	Amipro	3.0	2
Lotus	Organizer	2.1	3
Lotus	ccMail	6.0	3
Microsoft	Word	97	0
Microsoft	Explorer	4.1 (Win 98)	0

Continued

Office Continued

Vendor	Product	Version	Rating
Microsoft	Money	3.5	4
Microsoft	Word	2.0	2
Microsoft	Word	6.0	2
Microsoft	Access	2.0	3
Microsoft	Works	2.0a	3
Microsoft	Excel		0
Microsoft	Outlook	W16	0
Microsoft	Winfile	all 16-bit	4
Microsoft	Works-Spanish	3.0	5
Microsoft	Word Viewer	97 for Windows 16-bit	2
Modatech	Maximizer	1.2	3
Money Smith Systems	Money Smith	2.0	4
Netmanage	Ecco Pro	3.03	4
Nextbase	AutoRoute Express	3.02	2
Novell	Groupwise	5.2	0
On Technology	Meeting Maker	5.0.3	3
Oxford University Press	Concise Oxford Dictionary	2.0	5
Parsons Technology	Quickverse	3.0h	5
Postbank	GiroTel	1.3	4
Quark	Xpress	3.32	1
Random House	Unabridged Dictionary	CD-ROM	2
Richmond	Spanish-English Electronic Dictionary	4	SAP
SAPgui	4.0B	4	Symantec
Act for Windows	2.0.5	5	Visio Inc.
Visio	3.0	5	Word Place
Yeah Write	1.4	3	

Programming

Vendor	Product	Version	Rating
American Cybernetics	MultiEdit	7.11c	1
Borland	Pascal	7.0	3
Borland	Borland ResourceWorkshop	4.5	5
Borland	dBase	5.0	1
Inprise	Delphi	1.0	3
Micro Focus	Personal COBOL 2	V3.4	0
Microchip	MPLAB	4.12.00	4
Microsoft	Visual Basic	3.0	5
Microsoft	Visual Basic	3	2
Amzi	prolog	4.0	3

Win32 Applications

This section summarizes the performance of 32-bit applications under WINE.

A/V

Vendor	Product	Version	Rating
Adobe	After Effects	3.1	0
Adobe	Acrobat Reader	4.0	0
Apple	Quicktime	4.0	1
Asmith	Network	SCMPX	4
Bram Bros	HammerHead	1.0	1
Creative Labs	Creative Wave32	for AWE32	4
Creative Labs	Creative CD Player		3
Dragon Systems	NaturallySpeaking	3.0	0
Dragon Systems	Dragon Dictate	3.0	1
Goldenhawk	CDRWIN	3.6	4
Infinity Edge	Esprit	1.53	2
MMedia	Lview Pro	1.D2	4

Continued

A/V Continued

Vendor	Product	Version	Rating
Microsoft	CDPlayer	win95b (German)	2
Microsoft	Media Player	6.01.02.0217	2
ModPlug	ModPlug Tracker		2
NullSoft	WinAMP	2.091	2
NullSoft	WinAMP	1.72	3
NullSoft	WinAMP	2.22	2
NullSoft	WinAMP	1.92	3
NullSoft	WinAMP	2.04	3
NullSoft	WinAMP	1.80	4
NullSoft	WinAMP	2.091	3
Olivier Lapicque	ModPlugTracker	1.05	4
Real Networks	RealPlayer	G2	3
Real	RealPlayer	5.0	1
Real Networks	RealPlayer	7 beta	5
Resounding Technology	Roger Wilco	0.12p2	4
Sonic Foundry	Sound Forge	4.0d (build 173)	4
Syntrillium	Cool Edit	96	2
Tangerine / Agent Orange	Orangator	2.0	1
Vivo	VivoPowerPlayer	2.01	0
MIRC	mIRC	5.6	5
Rasmus Ekman	Granulab	0.99	5
Yamaha	soundVQ player	2.50b1	3

Graphics

Vendor	Product	Version	Rating
ACD Systems	ACDSee32	2.3	3
ACD Systems	ACDSee32	2.41	4
ADOBE	GoLive	4.0	0
AOL	AOLPress	2.0	4
Activeworlds.com	Active Worlds	2.1 Beta	3
Adobe	Photoshop	4	1

Vendor	Product	Version	Rating
Adobe	Streamline	3.01 demo	5
Adobe	Acrobat Distiller	3.01	5
Adobe	PageMaker	6.5	3
Adobe	PhotoShop	5.0	2
AutoDesk	AutoCAD	14	0
Caligari	TrueSpace	3.2	0
Caligari	TrueSpace	2.0	4
Caligari	TrueSpace	4.0	3
CambridgeSoft Corporation	ChemDrawPro	4.0.1	1
Cerious	ThumbsPlus	3.20	2
Confluent	Visual Thought	1.4	0
Corel	Corel Draw	4	2
Diehl Graphsoft	VectorWorks	8.0.0	2
Diehl Graphsoft	MiniCad	7.0	1
Firehand Technologies	Ember Ultra	3.11	1
Fractal Design	Painter	4.0	2
GlaxoWellcome	Raswin	2.6 beta-2a	2
Hamrick Software	VuePrint	6.1 pro/32	3
Hamrick Software	VuePrint	5.0, Pro/32	4
JASC	PaintShop Pro	5.0	0
JASC	PaintShop Pro	3.11	3
Kai Krause	Kai's Power Goo SE D		5
Live Picture	Live Pix	1.1	2
MGI	Photosuite SE SETM	1.05	0
Macromedia	Flash	3	2
Macromedia	Dreamweaver	2.1	2
Macromedia	Fireworks 2	2.x	0
Macromedia	Flash	4.0	1
MetaCreations	Bryce 3D	3.0	2
Metacreations	PowerGoo	1	3
MicroFluff	MSPaint	95	2
Micrografx	Picture Publisher	7	0

Continued

Graphics Continued

Vendor	Product	Version	Rating
Micrografx	PhotoMagic	4.0	1
Micrografx	Windows Draw	4.0	0
Microsoft	Directx Info	DX 5.0	4
Microsoft	dxsetup	5.0	4
Microsoft	Publisher	97	2
NewTek	Lightwave	5.5	5
Newtek	Aura	1.0	3
PolyBites	PolyView Beta	3.20b	4
ROM Tech	Vistapro	4.0	4
Real	Realplayer	G2 Plus	4
Robert McNeel & Assoc.	Rhino3D	1.0	1
Source View	SourceView Reader	3.64	4
Symantec	VisualPage	2.0	3
Topware	D-Sat	1	4
US Geological Survey	DLGV32	3.6	1
Ultra Fractal	Ultra Fractal	2.04	4
Vhorch software	PicCheck	3.0.7	4
Visio Corporation	Visio for Windows	4.0	1

Hardware

Vendor	Product	Version	Rating
Boulder Creek Engineering	Pod-A-Lyzer	2.1	4
Clavia	NordModular Editor	2.1	2
SynaptiCAD	VeriLogger	Pro	0

Network

Vendor	Product	Version	Rating
AOL	AOL Instant Messenger		4
AOL	AOL	4.0 (Win95 32-bit)	3
BTT Software	SNMP Trap Watcher	1.16	2

Vendor	Product	Version	Rating
Bio's Software	V console	2.3.1	3
BulletProof	Bullet Proof FTP	1.06	1
BulletProof	Bullet Proof FTP	1.13	2
CERA Belgium	CERA Online	2.0	4
CF	NetBus	1.70	5
CuteFTP	CuteFTP	2.01	1
Cyrusoft	Mulberry	1.4b2	1
Data Fellows	SSH for Win	1.1	4
David Harris	Pegasus Mail	3.x	3
Forte	Free Agent	1.11/32	4
FerretSoft	FileFerret	3.0000	1
GTE	Cirrus/DUATS	3.03	0
Hilgraeve	HyperTerminal	Private Edition 4.0	4
Hotline	PC Hotline	Beta	0
IBM/Lotus	Lotus Notes Client	4.5a	4
ICQ	ICQ 99a	99a	0
ICQ	ICQ v98	98	2
Info Interactive	Internet Call Manager		5
Ipswitch Inc.	WS_FTP LE	4.60	1
Juno	Juno	1.30	2
Lotus	Lotus Notes 4.5.2	W32 4.5.2b	3
Luu Tran	Xnews	2.11.08	4
MIRC	mIRC	5.5	1
Mark Hanson	XiRCON	1.0b4	3
Microsoft	Windows Terminal Server Client	4.0	1
Microsoft	Internet Explorer	4.0	0
Microsoft	Exchange Client	5.0	1
Microsoft	NetMeeting		2
Microsoft	Outlook Express	4.0.1	1
Microsoft	Internet Explorer	3.02	2
Microsoft	Windows95/FTP Client		5
Microsoft	telnet	1.0	5

Continued

Network Continued

Vendor	Product	Version	Rating
Microsoft	Internet Explorer	5.0 beta	1
Microsoft	Outlook Express	5	0
Mirabilis		ICQ	0
MIRC	mIRC	5.6	2
NASA	WinVN32 Newsgroup Viewer	wv32i999	3
NCS	Pirch98	1.0.1.1190	1
Net2Phone	Net2Phone	8.67	2
NetBus	NetBus		3
Novell	Netware Administrator	3X/95	0
Novell	GroupWise	5.5.0	0
NullSoft, Inc.	WinAMP	2.10	1
Opera	Opera Web Browser	3.21	2
Opera	Opera Web Browser	3.60	3
Pegasus	Pegasus Mail	3.0 Win NT/95	4
Qualcomm	Eudora Light	3.06	3
Qualcomm	Eudora Pro	4.2	2
SB Software	SB Newsbot	6.2	5
SoftArc	FirstClass Client	3.5	4
Sterling Commerce	GENTRAN:Server Workstation	5.1.0.4	2
Symantec	pcAnywhere 32	8.0	0
Tidewater Systems	WsFinger Client	1.7	5
Tribal	PowWow	3.7	0
Trontech	Newsgrabber	2.1.21	3
Universo Online	ComVC	1.0	2
Van Dyke Software	CRT	2.3	2
Yahoo	Messenger		0
Olitec	olicom	1.23	4

Office

Vendor	Product	Version	Rating
3Com	Palm Pilot	3.0	0
3D Studio	3D Studio Max		0
ACI	4D (Fourth Dimension)	6.0.6r3	2
Adobe	FrameMaker+SGML	5.5	0
Adobe	Distiller (PS-PDF)	3.0.1	4
Adobe	Exchange (PDF editor)	3.0.1	0
Blue Ocean	Track-It	3.0	5
Claris	FileMaker Pro	4.0v1	0
Claris	ClarisWorks	4.0	2
Corel	WordPerfect	8	0
Corel	WordPerfect	9	0
Counterpane Systems	Password Safe	1.7.1	5
Cygnus Productions	Password Coral	2.0.5	4
Datatech	MYOB Premier	1.1	2
David Harris	Pegasus Mail	3.1	2
Deltek Systems	Electronic Timesheet	2.4b.1	2
ES Computing	EditPlus	1.21	2
GoldMine Software	GoldMine for Windows 95	3.2	3
IBM	TranslationManager	2.5.0	2
Intuit	Quicken Deluxe 98	7.0	2
Intuit	Quicken 99 Deluxe		0
Intuit	QuickBooksPro (single-user)	6.0	1
Intuit	Quicken Home & Business 98	98	1
Intuit	QuickTax Deluxe	98	3
Intuit	QuickBooks Canada	5.0528	1
Intuit	Quicken 2000 Deluxe		3
Lotus	Notes	4.6a (International)	1
Lotus	Notes	4.6.2	4
Lotus	Approach	97.0	0
Lotus	Word Pro	9.0	0
MicroGrafx	FlowCharter	7.0	2

Continued

Office Continued

Vendor	Product	Version	Rating
Microcal	Origin	5.0	2
Microsoft	Encarta	98	0
Microsoft	Excel	95	2
Microsoft	Word	97	2
Microsoft	Wordpad		5
Microsoft	Money	5.0	0
Microsoft	PowerPoint	97	1
Microsoft	Access	97	0
Microsoft	Works	4.0 and 4.0a (32 bit)	0
Microsoft	Project	98	0
Microsoft	Notepad	95	3
Novell	Groupwise	5.2	0
On Communications	MeetingMaker		4
Sybase	Sybase ODBC/open Client	11.1	2
Visio	Visio Technical	4.1	1
Word Place, Inc	YeahWrite	1.5	2
efax	efax viewer		2

Programming

Vendor	Product	Version	Rating
Alan Phillips	Programmers File Editor	0.007.01	3
Allaire	HomeSite	3.0	1
Allaire	HomeSite	2.5	2
Allaire	Homesite	4.01	2
Allen Bradley	RSLogix 5	3.04	3
Borland	C++	5.0	1
Borland	C++Builder	3.0	1
Borland	Delphi	3.0	1
Borland	Jbuilder	2.0	0

Vendor	Product	Version	Rating
Borland	Conitec	Galep3	1.10
IDM Computer Solutions, Inc.	UltraEdit-32	6.10a	2
Inprise	Delphi	3	1
Inprise	Delphi	3.02	1
Inprise	Delphi	3.0	0
Inprise	Delphi	4.0	2
Inprise	Delphi	3.02	1
Inprise	Delphi	3.02	0
Macromedia	Dreamweaver	1.0	0
Macromedia	Dreamweaver	1.2	0
Macromedia	Dreamweaver	2.x	2
Microsoft	Visual Basic	6.0	0
Microsoft	Visual SourceSafe	5.0	0
Microsoft	Visual C++	5.0	1
Microsoft	Visual FoxPro	5.0	0
Microsoft	PowerPoint		4
Microsoft	Dependency Walker	1.0	3
Microsoft	Calculator	Win 3.10	5
Microsoft	ACPI Assembler	1.0.11	3
Microsoft	Visual C++	6	1
Microsoft	Visual Basic 5	5	3
Microsoft	Installshield	5.5	0
National Instruments	LabVIEW	5.0.1	0
National Instruments	LabVIEW	4.1	2
NetObjects	ScriptBuilder	3.0	0
Scriptics	Tcl/Tk	8.1	4
Sybase	Power Designor	6.0	0

Server

Vendor	**Product**	**Version**	**Rating**
Centura	SQLBase	7.51	3

Win32s Applications

This section summarizes the performance of 32-bit applications under WINE.

A/V

Vendor	Product	Version	Rating
MacroByte	VivoStatic	2.5	1
NullSoft	WinAMP	2.02	2

Graphics

Vendor	Product	Version	Rating
ACD Systems	ACDSee	2.3	0
ACD Systems	ACDSee	2.42	2
Adobe	Photo Deluxe		3
AutoDesk	Autocad	R12	1
Chrome-Imaging	Photonyx 1.5	1.5 beta	5
JASC	PaintShop Pro	5	0
JASC	PaintShop Pro	3.12	4
Microcal	Origin	5.0	2
Micrografx	Designer	7.0	0
Mitsubishi	DJ-1000 Viewer	1.00E	4
Newtek	Lightwave Modeler	5.5e	5
Visioneer	Paperport	5.0	1
MathSoft	MathCAD	6	3

Network

Vendor	Product	Version	Rating
AOL	AOL 4.0	4.0	0
AOL	AOL Instant Messenger		5

Vendor	Product	Version	Rating
BPFTP Software	Bullet Proof FTP	1.14	2
Excite	PAL – The Excite Messenger	1.11	4
Forte	Free Agent	1.0	4
Forte	Agent	1.6	4
Intel	Internet Sharing Client		1
Juno	Juno Email		2
KookaBurra Software	NetPal	1.2	0
Microsoft	Outlook Express 5	5.0	0
Microsoft	Internet Explorer	4.0	0
Mirabilis	ICQ 99A	99A	0
MIRC	mIRC	5.41	5
Opera Software	Opera Web Browser	3.6	4
Pegasus	Pegasus	3.01d	4
Qualcomm	Eudora	4	1
SB Software	SB News Robot	7.0	0

Office

Vendor	Product	Version	Rating
Lotus	123		0
Lotus	WordPro		0
Microsoft	Money 98	98 (6.0)	1
Microsoft	Office 97 Pro		0
Microsoft	Word	97	3
Microsoft	Word 97		3
Netscape	Communicator	4.6	1
Remedy	Aruser	3.0	4
Visio Inc.	Visio Technical	5.0	3

Programming

Vendor	Product	Version	Rating
Borland	Delphi 3	3	0
Borland	Borland C++		3
Borland	Borland C++	4.51	2
Borland	C++ Builder	3.0	1
Borland	Delphi 2.0		2
Wolfram	Mathematica	2.2.4	0
Wolfram	Mathematica	3.0	4

Graphics

Vendor	Product	Version	Rating
Autodesk	AutoCAD	R14.0	0

Network

Vendor	Product	Version	Rating
Checkpoint	Firewall-1 (GUI) Security Policy Editor	3.0b	1

Office

Vendor	Product	Version	Rating
Corel	WordPerfect		0
Lotus	Notes R5	5.0	3
Lotus	Notes	4.6.2 (Intl)	3
Microsoft	Word	97	0
Microsoft	Word	8	1

Programming

Vendor	Product	Version	Rating
AONIX	Software through Pictures	7.0	0
Borland/Inprise	Jbuilder 2	Prof Ed.	3
ParkPlace	VisualWorks	2.5	2

Miscellaneous Applications

In this section, which reflects entries in the WINE results database for applications that do not completely fit into any functional category, we sort only by vendor.

Miscellaneous Applications

Vendor	Product	Version	Rating
Academic Press	Gaint Molecules Application Polymer	1.0	3
Aladdin Systems	Stuffit Expander	1.0	4
Allaire	Homesite	3.0	1
Allaire	Homesite	4.0	0
Allen Resources	TestBank	4.0	5
Alpha Technologies	CDEX	1.20 Beta 5	1
Aptech Systems, Inc	Gauss for Windows NT/95	3.2.32	3
Autodesk	QuickCAD	6.0	0
Bremer Corporation	Notespad	8	0
Broderbund	Family Tree Maker	3.2	0
Broderbund	3D Home Architect Delux	2.1	2
BulletProof Software	BulletProof FTP	1.2	1
CBT Systems	Oracle & PowerSoft Training	98	3
Cambridge ChemSoft	ChemWeb	3.1	3
Addison-Wesley-Longman	LogicWorks 3 Interactive Circuit Design	3.01	3
Cheyenne	Bitware	3.30	0

Continued

Miscellaneous Applications Continued

Vendor	Product	Version	Rating
Coda	Finale	3.5.0r2	4
Commonwealth Bank (Australia)	NetBank	2	3
Cool-Edit	Cool-Wav		4
Counterpane Systems	Password Safe	1.1	2
Crocodile Clips Ltd	Crocodile Clips	3.2	5
Cyber Pass On-Line	CNE Quizzer	4.3	1
DATA BECKER	Skyplot Pro 95	95	3
DM	Money Maker	1.32	2
DeLorme	Street Atlas USA	6.0	1
DeLorme	AAA MapNGo	4.0	0
ESRI	ArcView	3.0a	0
FerretSoft	FileFerret		1
Furrer & Partner	PayMaker	2.01	4
GNU	WinCVS	1.06	5
GNU	Ntemacs	20.4	4
Helios Software Solutions	TextPad	3.2	1
INRIA	Scilab	2.4.1	4
Insanely Great Software	WinWeather 3.0	4.0	1
Intel	IParty Client	v1.0	3
Intel	IPartyd (server)	v1.0	4
Interactiv	Electronics Workbench	5.0	0
Intergaid	HyperReader	4.0	4
Intuit	Quick Books	5.0	0
Intuit	Quicken	3	5
Intuit	Quicken 98	7.0	4
Intuit	Quick Books Pro	5.0	3
JASC	Quick View Plus		0
LC Resources Inc.	Drylab For Windows	1.94	3
Lascaux Graphics	f(z), The Complex Variable Program		4
Logos Library Systems	Logos	2.1E	0
Macromedia	Director	5	0

Vendor	Product	Version	Rating
Maplesoft	Maple	V	3
Maplin	Catalogue	1.0	4
MathSoft	MathCAD Plus	5.0	3
MathSoft	MathCAD	7	1
Mathworks	Matlab	5.1	0
MicroCode Engineering	Circuit Maker	5	3
MicroFluff	File Manager	95	0
Microcal Software	Origin	3.5	4
Microsim	PSPICE DesignLab	6.1a	2
Microsoft	Multimedia Viewer	2.0	3
National Geographic Interactive	The Complete National Geographic		0
National Instruments	LabVIEW	5.0	0
NetObjects	Fusion	3	0
Nico Mak	winzip	7.0	3
Nico Mak	winzip	7.0 SR 1	2
NullSoft	WinAMP	2.04	3
OrCAD	Capture for Windows	7.10	0
Oxford University Press	French-English Dictionary		4
PKWARE	pkzip		4
Palladium Interactive	Ultimate Family Tree	2.4	0
Palm Computing (3com)	POSE (palm pilot emulator)	2.1	5
Parsons Technology	PC Bible Atlas		4
Parsons Technology	Bible Illustrator For Windows		4
Parsons Technology	Quickverse	4.0	4
Perwill	Mapper	6.03.20	4
Quark	Xpress3.31		2
RMS Technology, Inc.	Flightsoft Professional	1.57	3
SAS Institute	StatView	5	4
SETI @ Home	SETI @ Home	1.0	4
SK Computer Solutions	CodeBank	2.42	3
Sausage Software	HotDog16	2.57	0

Continued

Miscellaneous Applications Continued

Vendor	Product	Version	Rating
Security Dynamics	SoftID	1.2 RA2	2
Self Test Software	Big Red Self Test for Novell		1
Shape Software	ATOMS	4.1	4
Silver Mountain Software	TLG Workplace	5.0	3
SkyMap	SkyMap	3.1	3
Skyline Software	StarScape	1.5	5
Softham Enterprises	Signature Generator	1.2.2	3
Softkey	Infopedia	2.0	4
Softquad	HotMetal Pro	4	3
Softronics, Inc.	MultiMedia Logic	1.0	4
Southern Stars Software	SkyChart III	3.1	4
Symantec	pcANYWHERE	2.0	3
Syntrillium	Cool Edit Pro	1.2	0
Texas Instruments	WinLink	TI-86	3
Texas Instruments	TI-Graphlink		5
Timnathserah Inc	Online Bible	8.0	3
Virtual Reality Laboratories	Distant Suns	1.2	4
Waterloo Software	MapleV	4	2
Wiley-VCH	Biblio	32 Bit Edition, Release 1	3
Wolfram Research	Mathematica	2.2	1

Applications Rating a 5

Despite the WINE Project's instructions to the contrary, more than 200 tests of applications produced the highest possible rating. This section presents a selection of these applications, sorted only by vendor.

Applications Rating a 5

Vendor	Product	Version
AOL	Instant Messenger	Latest
Activision	Netstorm	5

Vendor	Product	Version
Adobe	Streamline	3
Adobe	Distiller	3.0
Aztech	FM-Radio Application	
Blizzard	StarCraft	1.0?
Blue Ocean	Track-It	3.0
Borland	Tdump	4.2.19.3 (BC 5.01)
Borland	Borland Resource Workshop	4.5
Bremer Corporation	Notespad 16	
Brodurbound	3D Home Architech	2.0
Bryce	Bryce 3D	3.0
CF NetBus	1.70	ChordWizard Software Pty Ltd
ChordWizard	1.5a	Chrome-Imaging
Photonyx	1.5 beta 2	5
Counterpane Systems	Password Safe	1.7.1
Crocodile Clips Ltd	Crocodile Clips	3.2
Epson	scanII	1.10E
Forte Inc	Free Agent	1.11
Info Interactive	Internet Call Manager	5
Intuit	Quicken For Windows	Version 3
Intuit	QuickTax	1999
Iomega	Zip drive software and driver	5.02
Ipswitch Inc.	WS_FTP Client	4.60
Kai Krause	Kai's Power Goo	SE D
Lotus	Lotus Notes	4.61a
Macromedia	Flash	4.0
Microlytics	Berlitz Interpreter	2.0.1
Microsoft	Wordpad	
Microsoft	Visual Basic	3.0
Microsoft	Regedit	4.0 (NT 4.0)
Microsoft	ftp client	W95
Microsoft	Telnet	1.0

Continued

Applications Rating a 5 Continued

Vendor	Product	Version
MIRC	mIRC	5.41
Netscape	Navigator Gold	v3.0
NewTek	Lightwave	5.5
Oxford University Press	Concise Oxford Dictionary	2.0
Real Networks	RealPlayer	7 beta
SB Software	SB Newsbot	6.2
SL/Waber	Electronic Bookmark for UPStart UPS units	1.2
Symantec	Act for Windows	2.0.5
Texas Instruments	TI-Graphlink	
Tidewater Systems	WsFinger Client	1.7
Visio Inc.	Visio	3.0

Applications Rating a 4

More than 600 tests in the WINE application performance database resulted in a rating of 4. That rating indicates that the application being tested ran substantially correctly, and was felt to be good enough for general use, with possible caveats. This section presents selections from this group, sorted only by vendor.

Applications Rating a 4

Vendor	Product	Version
ACD Systems	ACDSee32	2.41
AOL	AOL Instant Messenger	1.0.378
AOL	AOLPress	2.0 – 32bit
Ad Tools Inc.	Felix	
Adobe	Streamline	3
Adobe	Distiller	3.0
Adobe	Acrobat Reader	4.0
Aladdin Systems	Stuffit Expander	1.0

Vendor	Product	Version
Alchemy Mindworks	Graphic Workshop	1.1 (32bit)
Allen Resources	TestBank	4.0
Application Systems Heidelberg	MagiC_PC	1.10
Artec/Ultima	AS6E Scanner Driver	
Asmith Network	SCMPX	
Aztech	FM-Radio Application	
Beige Bag Software	B2Logic	3
Black Castle Software	UO Monitor	2.00a
Blue Ocean	Track-It	3.0
Borland	Turbo Pascal Windows	1.5
Borland	C++	4.5
Borland	TDump	4.2.19.3 (BC 5.01)
Borland	Borland Resource Workshop	4.5
Boulder Creek Engineering	Pod-A-Lyzer	2.1
Break Point Software	Hex WorksShop 32	2.10 32bit
Brodurbound	3D Home Architech	2.0
Bryce	Bryce 3D	3.0
CERA Belgium	CERA Online	2.0
CF	NetBus	1.70
Caligari	TrueSpace	2.0
Capilano Computing	LogicWorks	3
Checkfree	Checkfree	2.0
ChordWizard Software Pty Ltd	ChordWizard	1.5a
Chrome-Imaging	Photonyx 1.5	1.5 beta 2
Claris	FileMaker Pro	2.1
Coda	Finale	3.5.0r2
Cognitive Technology	Cuneiform	3.0
Cool-Edit	Cool-Wav	
Counterpane Systems	Password Safe	1.7.1
Creative Labs	Creative Wave32	AWE32
Crocodile Clips Ltd	Crocodile Clips	3.2
Cygnus Productions	Password Coral	2.0.5

Continued

Applications Rating a 4 Continued

Vendor	Product	Version
DDA	PhoneDisc (2nd Edition)	2.4.4
Data Fellows	SSH for Win	1.1
Data Tech	MYOB Test Drive	8
Epson	scanII	1.10E
Excite	Excite PAL	1.11ex (16-bit)
Forte	Free Agent	1.11/32
Forte	Agent16	v1.5
Forte	Agent32	1.5
Furrer & Partner	PayMaker	2.01
GNU	NTemacs	20.4
Ghisler Software	Windows Commander	4.01
Goldenhawk	CDRWIN	3.6
Group 42	GraphX Viewer	1.51 (16-bit)
Hamrick Software	VuePrint	5.0, Pro/32
Hermeneutika	Bibleworks	3.5
Hewlett Packard	HP PE/ME10 for Windows	7.1
Hilgraeve	HyperTerminal Private Edition	4.0
IBM	Home Director	
INRIA	Scilab	2.4.1
Info Interactive	Internet Call Manager	
Inprise	VisiBroker	3.3 (JAVA)
Intel	Ipartyd (server)	v1.0
Intergaid	HyperReader	4.0
Intuit	QuickBooks Pro	5.0d
Intuit	Quicken Deluxe	4.0
Intuit	Quicken 98 Deluxe	7.0
Intuit	QuickTax	1999
Iomega	Zipdrive software and driver	5.02
Ipswitch Inc.	WS_FTP Client	4.60
J.Lin	Speedy	1.1
JASC	Media Center 2	2.02
Kai Krause	Kai's Power Goo	SE D

Vendor	Product	Version
Kiplinger	TaxCut	97
Kith and Kin	SPANSOFT	3.1
Lascaux Graphics	f(z), The Complex Variable Program	
Linguistic Systems	Euroglot Professional	3.0
Lotus	Notes	4.5.2b
Lotus	Notes	4.6.2
Luu Tran	Xnews	2.11.08
MIRC	mIRC	5.5
Mmedia	Lview Pro	1.D2
Macromedia	Flash	4.0
Maplin	Catalogue	1.0
Mathworks	Matlab	5.1
Microcal Software	Origin	3.5
Microchip	MPASM for Windows	2.20
Microchip	MPLAB	4.12.00
Microlytics	Berlitz Interpreter	2.0.1
Microsoft	Calc	n/a
Microsoft	WinAMP	1.72
Microsoft	Bookshelf	95
Microsoft	Developer Network Info Browser	96
Microsoft	Internet Explorer	3.03
Microsoft	Frontpage Express	2.0.2.1118
Microsoft	Wordpad	1.0
Microsoft	Excel	5.0
Microsoft	WinDiff	
Microsoft	Money	3.5
Microsoft	Windows Terminal Server Client	4.0
Microsoft	Visual Basic	3.0
Microsoft	Directx Info (dxinfo)	DX 5.0
Microsoft	dxsetup	DirectX 5.0
Microsoft	Regedit	4.0 (NT4.0)
Microsoft	ftp client	W95

Continued

Applications Rating a 4 Continued

Vendor	Product	Version
Microsoft	PowerPoint File Viewer	
Microsoft	Works-Spanish	3.0
Microsoft	Excel	97
Microsoft	Encarta	99
Microsoft	BookShelf	98
Microsoft	Automap Streets	1995
Mindscape	Grolier Encyclopedia 95	7.03
Mitsubishi	DJ-1000 Viewer	1.00E
Modeltech	Vsystem	4.6e
Money Smith Systems	Money Smith	2.0
National Instruments	LabVIEW	4.1
Netmanage	Ecco Pro	3.03
Netscape	Navigator Gold (16bit)	3.01
Netscape	Navigator (32-bit)	3.01
Netscape	Communicator	4.6
NewTek	Lightwave 5.5	5.5
NewsXpress	nx	1.0b4
Newtek	Lightwave Modeler	5.5e
NullSoft	WinAMP	1.73
Olivier Lapicque	ModPlugTracker	1.05
On Technology	Meeting Maker	5.0.3
Opera	Opera Web Browser	3.60
Oxford University Press	Concise Oxford Dictionary	2.0
Oxford University Press	French-English Dictionary	
PKWARE	pkzip	
Palm Computing (3com)	POSE (Palm Pilot Emulator)	2.1
Parsons Technology	PC Bible Atlas	
Parsons Technology	Bible Illustrator For Windows	
Parsons Technology	Quickverse	4.0
Parsons Technology	Quickverse	3.0h
Perwill	Mapper	6.03.20
PolyBites	PolyView	3.20b
Project Pluto	Guide	7.0 (16 Bit)

Vendor	Product	Version
Protel	Advanced PCB	2.7
Qualcomm	Eudora Light	1.5.2
Qualcomm	Eudora Pro	4.2
ROM Tech	Vistapro	4.0
Real	Realplayer	G2 Plus
RealSoft	Real3D	3.5
Remedy	Notifier	3.0
Remedy	ARuser	3.2.1
RevCan	WinTOD	99
Richmond	Richmond Spanish-English Electronic Dictionary	
Roger Sayle	RasWin	2.6
SAP	SAPgui	4.0B
SAS Institute	StatView	5
SB Software	SB Newsbot	6.2
SETI@home	SETI @ HOME client	win32 GUI client 1.06
SL/Waber	Electronic Bookmark for UPStart UPS units	1.2
Scriptics	Tcl/Tk	8.1
Softarc	First Class Client	3.1
Softkey	Infopedia	2.0
Softkey	American Heritage Dictionary	3
SoftQuad	HoTMetaL Pro	2.0
Softronics, Inc.	MultiMedia Logic	1.0
Software by Design	TxEdit	3.8
Sonic Foundry	Sound Forge XP	3.0d
Source View	SourceView Reader	3.64
Southern Stars Software	SkyChart III	3.1
Symantec	Act for Windows	2.0.5
Texas Instruments	WinTach	1.2
Texas Instruments	TI-Graphlink	
Tidewater Systems	WsFinger Client	1.7
USR/3Com	Modem Upgrade Wizard	

Continued

Applications Rating a 4 Continued

Vendor	Product	Version
Vandyke	SecureCRT	2.4
Vhorch Software	PicCheck	3.0.7
Visio	Visio Technical	4.1 (16-bit)
Waterloo	Maple V	R4
White Harvest	Seedmaster	3.1a
TommySoftware	Tek Illustrator	3.15

Applications Rating a 3

More than 900 tests in the WINE application performance database resulted in a rating of 3. That rating indicates that applications had sufficient functionality for noncritical work, but crashed on occasion, demonstrated setup problems, required patches, and so on. This section presents selections from this group which pertain only to Win32 systems. Those selections are sorted only by vendor.

Applications Rating a 3

Vendor	Product	Version
ACD Systems	ACDSee32	2.3
ACD Systems	ACDSee32	2.41
AOL	AOL Instant Messenger	1.0.378
Academic Press	Gaint Molecules Application Polymer	1.0
Activision	Netstorm	
Ad Tools Inc.	Felix	
Adept Computer Solutions	Street Maps USA	V6.00.11
Adobe	Streamline	3
Adobe	FrameMaker	4
Adobe	Distiller	3.0
Adobe	Acrobat Reader	2.1
Adobe	PhotoShop	4.01 w/MMX
Adobe	Acrobat Reader	4.0

Vendor	Product	Version
Aladdin Systems	Stuffit Expander	1.0
Alan Phillips	Programmers File Editor	0.007.01
Alchemy Mindworks	Graphic Workshop	1.1 (32-bit)
Alchemy Mindworks	GIF Construction Set	1.0Q
Alexander Simonic	WinEdt	1.414
Allen Bradley	RSLogix 5	3.04
Allen Resources	TestBank	4.0
Alliare	HomeSite	2.5
AlphaSoft	Wörterbuch	1994
American Cybernetics	Multi-edit	7.11c1
Appgen	PowerWindows Client	4.1
Application Systems Heidelberg	MagiC_PC	1.10
Applied Computing Services	Computer Harpoon for Windows	1.3
Aptech Systems, Inc	Gauss for Windows NT/95	3.2.32
Artec/Ultima	AS6E Scanner Driver	4
Asmith Network	SCMPX	4
Audioactive	Player	1.3
Autodesk	AutoCAD	LT 97
Aztech	FM-Radio Application	
Beige Bag Software	B2Logic	3
Berlitz Publishing	Berlitz Interpreter	2
Bertelsmann	Discovery	97
Bio's Software	V console	2.3.1
Borland	C++	5.0
Borland	Turbo Pascal Windows	1.5
Borland	C++	4.5
Borland	Borland C++	3.1
Borland	Pascal for Windows	7.0
Borland	Tdump	4.2.19.3 (BC 5.01)
Borland	Borland Resource Workshop	4.5
Borland/Inprise	Jbuilder 2 Prof. Ed. Command Line Tools	2 Prof. Ed.

Continued

Applications Rating a 3 Continued

Vendor	Product	Version
Boulder Creek Engineering	Pod-A-Lyzer	2.1
Break Point Software	Hex WorksShop 32	2.10 32bit
Bremer Corporation	Notespad 16	
Broadgun Software	Arc-It-Up	1.0
Brodurbound	3D Home Architech	2.0
Bryce	Bryce 3D	3.0
C.M.Western, Uni Bristol	pgopher	pg32v373
CA	Simply Money	
CBT Systems	Oracle & PowerSoft Training	98
CERA Belgium	CERA Online	2.0
CF	NetBus	1.70
COGNOS	PowerPlay Transformer	6.0
Caligari	trueSpace	2.0
Caligari	trueSpace	4.0
Cambridge ChemSoft	ChemWeb	3.1
Capilano Computing / Addison-Wesley-Longman	LogicWorks 3 Interactive Circuit Design	3.01
Cayenne Software Inc.	ClassDesigner	1.1.4
Centura Software	SQLBase	7.51
Cerious Software	ThumbsPlus	2.0a
Cetus Software	CwordPad	1.2
Checkfree	Checkfree	2.0
ChordWizard Software Pty Ltd	ChordWizard	1.5a
Chrome-Imaging	Photonyx	1.5
Claris	File Maker Pro	2.1
Coda	Finale	3.5.0r2
Coda	Finale	2.2
Cognitive Technology	Cuneiform	3.0
Commonwealth Bank (Australia)	NetBank	2
Conitec	Galep3	1.10
Cool-Edit	Cool-Wav	4
Corel	Draw	3.0
Corel	WordPerfect	8

Vendor	Product	Version
Counterpane Systems	Password Safe	1.7.1
Creative Labs	Creative Wave32 (for AWE32)	
Creative Labs	Creative CD Player	
Creative Wonders	Sesame Street Learning Series	
Crocodile Clips Ltd	Crocodile Clips	3.2
CuteFTP	CuteFTP 16-bit	2.0
CuteFTP	CuteFTP	2.6
Cygnus Productions	Password Coral	2.0.5
DATA BECKER	Skyplot Pro	95
DATA BECKER	Skyplot	95
DDA	PhoneDisc (2nd Edition)	2.4.4
Data Fellows	SSH for Win	1.1
Data Tech	MYOB Test Drive	8
DeScribe Corp.	DeScribe Word Processor	5.0/Windows 16-bit
Epson	scanII	1.10E
Excite	Excite PAL	1.11ex (16-bit)
Forte	Free Agent	1.11/32
Forte	Agent	1.5
Forte	Agent	1.7
Furrer & Partner	PayMaker	2.01
GNU	WinCVS	1.06
GNU	NTemacs	20.4
Ghisler Software	Windows Commander	4.01
GoldMine Software	GoldMine for Windows 95	3.2
Goldenhawk	CDRWIN	3.6
Group 42	GraphX Viewer	1.51 (16-bit)
Hamrick Software	VuePrint	6.1 pro/32
Hamrick Software	VuePrint	5.0, Pro/32
Hermeneutika	Bibleworks	3.5
Hewlett Packard	HP PE/ME10 for Windows	7.1
Hilgraeve	HyperTerminal Private Edition	4.0
IBM	IBM Home Director	

Continued

Applications Rating a 3 Continued

Vendor	Product	Version
IDM Computer Solutions	UltraEdit	6.10
INRIA Internet Call Manager	Scilab	2.4.1Info Interactive
Inprise	Delphi	1.0
Inprise	VisiBroker	3.3 (JAVA)
Intel	IParty Client	v1.0
Intel	IPartyd (server)	v1.0
Intergaid	HyperReader	4.0
Intuit	QuickBooks Pro	5.0d
Intuit	Quicken Deluxe	3.0
Intuit	Quicken	4.0
Intuit	Quicken 98 Deluxe	7.0
Intuit	Quicken For Windows	3
Intuit	Quicken	6
Intuit	Quicken	2000 Deluxe
Intuit	QuickTax	1999
Iomega	Zipdrive software and driver	5.02
Ipswitch Inc.	WS_FTP Client	4.60
Ipswitch Inc.	WS_FTP Limited Edition	3.10
Itautec	Redação da Lingua Portuquesa	any
JASC	Paint Shop Pro	3.11
JASC	Paint Shop Pro	3.12
JASC	Media Center	2.02
Juno	Juno	1.30
KMSystems	UTS Express	2.1
Kai Krause	Kai's Power Goo	SE D
Kiplinger	TaxCut	97
Klicksoft	KlickTel Deutschland	98
Knowledge Adventure	Dinosaur Adventure 3D	4.0
LC Resources Inc.	Drylab For Windows	1.94
Lascaux Graphics	f(z), The Complex Variable Program	
Linguistic Systems	Euroglot Professional	3.0

Vendor	Product	Version
Lotus	Notes	4.11a
Lotus	1-2-3	5
Lotus	Improv	2.0
Lotus	Notes 4.5.2	4.5.2b
Lotus	Notes	4.6.2
Lotus	Organizer	2.1
Lotus	ccMail	6.0
Lotus	Notes	4.6.3
Lotus	Notes	5.0
Luu Tran	Xnews	2.11.08
MIRC	mIRC	5.5
Macromedia	Flash	3.0
Macromedia	Flash	4.0
Maplesoft	Maple	V
Maplin	Catalogue	1.0
MathSoft	MathCAD Plus	5.0
Mathworks	Matlab	5.1
MetaCreations	Bryce4	
Metacreations	PowerGoo	1
MicroCode Engineering	Circuit Maker	5
Microcal Software	Origin	3.5
Microcal Software	Origin	4.0
Microchip	MPASM for Windows	2.20
Microchip	MPLAB	4.12.00
Microlytics	Berlitz Interpreter	2.0.1
Microsoft	Works	2
Microsoft	Calc	n/a
Microsoft	Visual Basic	3.0
Microsoft	Notepad	95
Microsoft	Bookshelf	95
Microsoft	Developer Network Info Browser	96
Microsoft	Encarta	96

Continued

Applications Rating a 3 Continued

Vendor	Product	Version
Microsoft	Internet Explorer 3.03 (16 bit)	3.03
Microsoft	Excel	97
Microsoft	Frontpage Express	2.0.2.1118
Microsoft	Wordpad	1.0
Microsoft	Helpfile viewer	32-bit
Microsoft	Excel	5.0
Microsoft	WinDiff	5
Microsoft	Money	3.5
Microsoft	Windows Terminal Server Client	4.0
Microsoft	Access	2.0
Microsoft	Wordpad	
Microsoft	Directx Info (dxinfo)	DX 5.0
Microsoft	dxsetup	DirectX 5.0
Microsoft	Telnet	3.1
Microsoft	Regedit	4.0 (NT4.0 Version)
Microsoft	Windows95/ftp client	
Microsoft	PowerPoint File Viewer	
Microsoft	Dependency Walker	1.0
Microsoft	Visual SourceSafe	5.0
Microsoft	Works-Spanish	3.0
Microsoft	Multimedia Viewer	2.0
Microsoft	ACPI Assembler	1.0.11
Microsoft	Exchange Client	5.0 16-bit
Microsoft	Visual Basic 5	Enterprise Edition
Microsoft	Paint	
Microsoft	Internet Explorer	4.0
Microsoft	Automap Streets	
Mindscape	Grolier Encyclopedia 95	7.03
Mitsubishi	DJ-1000 Viewer	1.00E
Modatech	Maximizer	1.2
Money Smith Systems	Money Smith	2.0

Vendor	Product	Version
Mustek	Scanner Solutions	600 III
NASA	WinVN32 Newsgroup Viewer	wv32i999
NS / EDS	NS Reisplanner	1998.2
National Instruments	LabVIEW	4.1
NetBus	NetBus	1998
Netmanage	Ecco Pro	3.03
Netscape	Navigator Gold (16bit)	3.01
Netscape	Navigator (32-bit)	3.01
Netscape	Communicator	4.6
NewTek	Lightwave Modeler	5.5e
Newtek	Aura	1.0
Nico Mak	Winzip	7.0
Nico Mak	Winzip Self-Extractor	2.1
Novell	GroupWise	5.2
NullSoft	WinAMP	2.04
Olivier Lapicque	ModPlugTracker	1.05
Olivier Lapique	Modplug Player	1.4
On Technology	Meeting Maker	5.0.3
Opera	Opera Web Browser	3.60
Origin Systems	Ultima Online	1.26.1
Oxford University Press	Concise Oxford Dictionary	2.0
Oxford University Press	French-English dictionary	
PCN	Pointcast	2.5
PKWARE	pkzip	
PKware	PkZip for Windows	2.50
Palm Computing (3com)	POSE (palm pilot emulator)	2.1
Parsons Technology	PC Bible Atlas	
Parsons Technology	Bible Illustrator For Windows	
Parsons Technology	Quickverse	4.0
Parsons Technology	Quickverse	3.0h
Peanut Software	WinFeed – fractal exploration program	1999
Perwill	Mapper	6.03.20

Continued

Applications Rating a 3 Continued

Vendor	Product	Version
Peanut Software	WinArc	1999
Pegasus	Pegasus Mail	3.0 Win NT/95
Protel	Advanced PCB	2.7
Qualcomm	Eudora Light	3.01 16-bit
Qualcomm	Eudora Light	3.06
Qualcomm	Eudora Pro	4.2
RMS Technology, Inc.	Flightsoft Professional	1.57
ROM Tech	Vistapro	4.0
RT Systems, Inc	ICOM programmer	IC-T7A, IC-W32, and IC-T2A
Real	RealPlayer	G2 Plus
Remedy	Aruser	3.0
Remedy	Notifier	3.0
RevCan	WinTOD	99
Richmond	Spanish-English Electronic Dictionary	
SAP	SAPgui	4.0B
SAS Institute	StatView	
SB Software	SB Newsbot	6.2
SK Computer Solutions	CodeBank	2.42
SL/Waber	Electronic Bookmark for UPStart UPS units	1.2
Scriptics	Tcl/Tk	8.1
Silver Mountain Software	TLG Workplace	5.0
Sky Scan	Digidome	2.0
SkyMap	SkyMap	3.1
Skyline Software	StarScape for Windows 3.X	1.5
SoftArc	FirstClass Client	5.5
Softarc	First Class Client	3.1
Softham Enterprises	Signature Generator	1.2.2
Softkey	Infopedia	2.0
Softkey International	American Heritage Dictionary	3

Softqaud	HoTMetaL Pro	2.0
Softquad	HoTMetaL Pro	4
Softronics, Inc.	MultiMedia Logic	1.0
Softronix, INC	MSWLogo	6.4f
Software by Design	TxEdit	3.8
Sonic Foundry	Sound Forge XP	3.0d
Source View	SourceView Reader	3.64
Southern Stars Software	SkyChart III	3.1
Spry	Imagevw	
SuperKey	SuperMap USA	
Symantec	VisualPage	2.0
Symantec	Act for Windows	2.0.5
Symantec	pcANYWHERE	2.0
Texas Instruments	WinTach	1.2
Texas Instruments	WinLink	TI-86
Texas Instruments	TI-Graphlink Software	
Tidewater Systems	WsFinger Client	1.7
Timnathserah Inc	Online Bible	8.0
Tivoli	Tivoli Desktop	3.2
Transcender	NTcert 4.0, MCSE certification	4.0
Trontech	Newsgrabber	2.1.21
USR/3Com	Modem Upgrade Wizard	
Ultra Fractal	Ultra Fractal	2.04
Vandyke	SecureCRT	2.4
Visio	Visio Technical	4.1 (16-bit)
Visio	Visio	3.0
Visio Inc.	Visio Technical	5.0
White Harvest	Seedmaster	3.1a
Wiley-VCH	Biblio	32 Bit /R1
Wolfram Research	Mathematica	3.0
Word Place	YeahWrite	1.4
Word Place	YeahWrite	1.5

Workable Office Applications

This last summary section presents office applications that earned a rating of 3 or higher, sorted only by vendor.

Workable Office Applications

Vendor	Product	Version
3COM	Total Control Manager	5.5.1 / 6.0.x
ACD Systems	ACDSee32	2.3
ACD Systems	ACDSee32	2.41
AOL	AOL Instant Messenger	4
AOL	AOLPress	2.0
Academic Press	Gaint Molecules Application Polymer	1.0
Adobe	Distiller (PS-PDF)	3.0.1
Adobe	PageMaker	6.5
Adobe	PhotoShop	4.01 w/MMX
Adobe	Acrobat Reader 4.0	4.0
Aladdin Systems	Stuffit Expander	1.0
Alan Phillips	Programmers File Editor	0.007.01
Alexander Simonic	WinEdt	1.414
Allen Bradley	RSLogix 5	3.04
Asmith Network	SCMPX	
Bio's Software	V console	2.3.1
Boulder Creek Engineering	Pod-A-Lyzer	2.1
Broderbund	3D Home Architech	2.0
CBT Systems	Oracle & PowerSoft Training	September 98
CERA belgium	CERA online	2.0
Caligari	trueSpace	2.0
Centura Software	SQLBase	7.51
ChordWizard Software Pty Ltd	ChordWizard	1.5a
Commonwealth Bank (Australia)	NetBank	2
Conitec	Galep3	1.10
Counterpane Systems	Password Safe	1.7.1
Data Fellows	SSH for Win	1.1

Vendor	Product	Version
Data Tech	MYOB Test Drive	8
Eugene Roshal	WinRAR95	2.05
Forte	Free Agent	1.11/32
GNU	WinCVS	1.06
GNU	NTemacs	20.4
GoldMine Software	GoldMine for Windows 95	3.2
Hamrick Software	VuePrint	6.1 pro/32
Hilgraeve	HyperTerminal Private	4.0
INRIA	Scilab	2.4.1
Info Interactive	Internet Call Manager	
Intel	IParty Client	v1.0
Intel	IPartyd (server)	v1.0
Intuit	Quicken 98 Deluxe	7.0
Intuit	QuickTax Deluxe	98
Intuit	QuickBooksPro	5.0
Intuit	Quicken	2000 Deluxe
Intuit	Quicken	99 Deluxe
JASC	PaintShop Pro	3.11
Juno Software	Juno	1.30
KMSystems	UTS Express	2.1
Kai Krause	Kai's Power Goo	SE D
LC Resources Inc.	Drylab For Windows	1.94
Linguistic Systems	Euroglot Professional	3.0
Lotus	Lotus Notes	4.5.2b
Lotus	Notes	4.6.2
Luu Tran	Xnews	2.11.08
MIRC	mIRC	5.5
Macromedia	Flash	3.0
Macromedia	Flash	4.0
Maplesoft	Maple	V
Mathworks	Matlab	5.1
MicroCode Engineering	Circuit Maker	5

Continued

Workable Office Applications Continued

Vendor	Product	Version
Microsoft	WinDiff	5
Microsoft	Calculator	Win 3.10
Microsoft	Wordpad	
Microsoft	Word	97
Microsoft	Directx Info (dxinfo)	DX 5.0
Microsoft	dxsetup	DirectX 5.0
Microsoft	Excel	97
Microsoft	Regedit	4.0/NT4.0
Microsoft	Encarta	97
Microsoft	Windows95/ftp client	
Microsoft	PowerPoint File Viewer	
Microsoft	Telnet	1.0
Microsoft	Dependency Walker	1.0
Microsoft	Visual SourceSafe	5.0
Microsoft	ACPI Assembler	1.0.11
Microsoft	Notepad	95
Microsoft	BookShelf	98
Microsoft	Visual Basic 5 (SP3)	5
Microsoft	File Manager	98
Microsoft	Internet Explorer	5
Microsoft	Paint	
Microsoft	Powerpoint	2000
Microsoft	Internet Explorer	4.0
Mustek	Scanner Solutions 600	
NASA	WinVN32 Newsgroup Viewer	wv32i999
Nico Mak	winzip	7.0
NullSoft	WinAMP	2.04
Olivier Lapicque	ModPlugTracker	1.05
Olivier Lapique	Modplug Player	1.4
On Communications	MeetingMaker	4
Opera	Opera Web Browser	3.60

Vendor	Product	Version
PKWARE	pkzip	
Pegasus	Pegasus Mail	3.0 Win NT/95
Qualcomm	Eudora Light	3.06
Qualcomm	Eudora Pro	4.2
RT Systems, Inc	ICOM programmer	3
Real	RealPlayer	G2 plus
SETI @ Home	SETI @ Home	1.0
SK Computer Solutions	CodeBank	2.42
Scriptics	Tcl/Tk	8.1
Silver Mountain	TLG Workplace	5.0
SoftArc	FirstClass Client	5.5
Softham	Signature Generator	1.2.2
Softkey	Infopedia	2.0
Softquad	HoTMetaL Pro	4
Sonic Foundry	Sound Forge	4.0d (build 173)
Source View	SourceView Reader	3.64
Southern Stars	SkyChart III	3.1
Symantec	VisualPage	2.0
Texas Instruments	TI-Graphlink Software	5
Tidewater Systems	WsFinger Client	1.7
Timnathserah Inc	Online Bible	8.0
Tivoli	Tivoli Desktop	3.2
Trontech	Newsgrabber	2.1.21
Ultra Fractal	Ultra Fractal	2.04
Vandyke	SecureCRT	2.4
Waterloo Maple	Maple V	R4
Wiley-VCH	Biblio	32-bit Edition

Appendix C

Summary of Tips and Cautions

Tips Summary

We've organized this section into the same topic areas used as chapter titles. Only those Tips we feel to be most important to quick problem-solving appear here.

Requirements

Software requirements:

- At the time this book was being written, pre-compiled WINE binaries for Red Hat Linux 6.x were in preparation but not yet complete.
- Any X libraries that were compiled under the glibc2 GNU will be reentrant and therefore will support multithreading. Further, multithreading is supported by all versions of Linux released in 1999.

Hardware requirements:

- In addition to the SCSI controllers outlined in Table 1-2, there are dozens of others, from a variety of manufacturers, that coexist quite easily with most Intel Unix versions. If you plan to use SCSI as part of your WINE implementation, check the documentation for your operating system to find alternatives to the cards noted in the table.

- Table 1-4 covers only a few percent of the video adapters with which PC Unix will work. For the most complete list, go to http://www.xfree86.org/cardlist.txt.

- Even some fully Sound Blaster–compatible cards may not work with some Intel Unix versions. If your audio adapter uses an ASP chip set or offers specialized MIDI effects, it may present problems to the OS.

Installation

Commercial availability:

- When this book went to press, WINE was available as part of two commercial Linux distributions: SuSE and Caldera.

wine.conf:

- The WINE Project recommends using win95 to emulate any of ext2fs, VFAT and FAT32, and specifying msdos only if you *must* simulate a FAT16 file system. Further, the project urges no use of the value unix for the fstype argument unless you intend to port applications to WINE by using its library WINELIB, avoiding FAT16, and relying primarily on the win95 fstype.

- The WINE Project advises us *not* to specify loading the kernel, kernel32, gdi, gdi32, user, or user32 modules as anything other than built in DLLs. Failing to observe this caution may cause WINE to fail, since the suite cannot work with native Windows versions of these libraries. Nor do the members of the Project anticipate that WINE in its native version will ever be able to use kernel32. As a result, there is usually no need to change the DLLOverrides section of wine.conf.

- The WINE Project points out that defining DLL pairings does not guarantee either that the pairs in question will in fact be loaded as the same type of DLL or that correct versions of either member of the pair will be loaded. The team suggests, as a result, that the DLLPairs section be left unaltered. Note also that this section header and any values included under it may not be present in future versions of WINE.

- The WINE Project recommends ensuring that DLL pairs, such as comdlg32 and commdlg, have exactly the same load order, so as to preclude runtime errors that might result from mismatches between the versions of related libraries.

- The WINE Project recommends using the native version of avifile, the Audio Video Interleave, an audio/video standard developed by Microsoft but not yet fully implemented in WINE.

- The WINE Project recommends using the WINE implementation of GDI32 DLL. Supplying the =n parameter to this option/name combination at the command line can create rather than resolve problems; the native version of GDI32 and WINE cannot work together.

- Note that, while they are not supported explicitly by means of separate parameters to the winver option, most applications that ordinarily run under Windows 98 or Windows 2000 will perform properly if the win95 parameter is given to winver. That's because this option simply changes the OS version number reported to applications.

Advanced Compilation and Configuration

DLL load order:

- WINE's default DLL load order follows this algorithm: for all DLLs that have a fully functional WINE implementation, or where the native DLL is known not to work, the built-in library will be loaded first. In all other cases, the native DLL takes load-order precedence.

debugmsg:

- Specifying the TRACE class with debugmsg may produce far too much output.

- Don't be confused by the apparent inconsistent use of case in discussing classes of WINE messages. When working at the command line, supply names such as trace in lower case. But expect to see them rendered in upper case when consulting much of the documentation from the WINE project.

- FIXME and ERR message classes are enabled by default, while the TRACE and WARN classes are disabled by default.

- A channel name can represent either a complete DLL or a single API. Names must be supplied to WINE at startup with the same spelling and in the same case in which they appear in WINE's list of such names, which is in turn created during compilation.

- Redirect debugmsg's output to a file precisely because that output can be so large. debugmsg frequently produces several megabytes.

- Consider combining redirection of debugmsg's output to a file with using operating system commands such as head, tail, grep, or split, in order to produce diagnostics of more manageable size.

Fonts and font conversion:

- bdftopcf, a font compiler that frequently acts as a font format conversion utility, can convert font files from the Bitmap Distribution Format to the Portable Compiled Format. The latter format can be read by several hardware architectures while at the same time allowing the specification of a particular architecture that can read font files directly, without any reformatting. Such a scheme improves performance on the specified machine, while ensuring at the same time that font files will remain portable.

- If you create a new font directory for converted fonts, be sure to add that new directory's name to the font path.

- mkfontdir creates an index of a directory's X font files.

- xset is a utility that allows you to establish user display-related preferences under X.

- Be aware that while WINE doesn't require such fonts, its look and feel can be improved by fonts that the X server with which it runs prefers.

- Some applications try to load custom fonts as they launch; Word 6.0 for Windows is one such app. As a result, WINE may display a message of this sort. Simply convert any font files indicated in such messages.

```
STUB: AddFontResource( SOMEFILE.FON )
```

- TrueType fonts aren't easily rendered. Although there are several commercial applications that can convert them, the quality of the results is far from stellar according to members of the WINE Project, who suggest, as an alternative, using a font server capable of rendering TrueType fonts.

- Before you make any aliasing additions to wine.conf, be sure that the X font to which your edits refer actually exists. Use the X utility xfontsel, a program that can display the names of all fonts known to your X server, to examine samples of each, or retrieve the full name for a font.

- However font conversion and aliasing are carried out, WINE will ignore font aliases if it determines that a correct native X font is available.

- WINE uses its font metrics file to rebuild font dimensions from scratch when it detects changes in the X font configuration.

Interoperability and Interconnectivity Issues

SMB:

- SMB operates as a client/server, request/response protocol, meaning that the client, by initiating exchanges with requests to the server, is in effect in control of such exchanges. One exception exists to this rule of thumb. Should a client have requested a file in a locked mode, and the responding server, after granting that request, receive a subsequent request for the same file from another client, the original lock will be broken by the server, and an unsolicited message sent to the client informing it of the broken lock.

- Should they operate in TCP/IP environments, SMB clients must actually use NetBIOS over TCP/IP to make their initial connection.

- When either TCP/IP or NetBEUI makes the initial SMB connection, it is the NetBIOS API that actually does the work. Microsoft refers to such connections as both NBT and NetBT in others, and calls NetBEUI-based SMB connections NBF.

Samba:

- Note that Samba's default home in the file system, /usr/local/, also houses WINE. Keep this in mind when anticipating how much free disk space installing Samba in addition to WINE will require.

smb.conf:

- Like WINE, Samba indicates all section headers in its configuration file with square bracket pairs ([ ]).

- Extensive changes to smb.conf, such as those needed to provide sharing of specific directories, the use of passwords, and printing, are best accomplished by means of the Samba utility called swat. swat, a scaled-down Web server, responds to HTTP connections on port 901. swat provides a graphical interface for configuring Samba and for some of Samba's documentation. To connect to swat, just start your browser and point it at `http://localhost:901`.

- Sections within smb.conf, and therefore shares, may be set up as guest services, which require no password, but rather rely on a server OS guest account to define access privileges. In any case, a Samba server cannot grant more access than its host OS permits.

- If guest access is specified in the [homes] section of smab.conf, all home directories will be visible to all clients, *without a password.* Therefore, should such access be configured, it should be accompanied by the specification of read-only mode.

- By default, Samba 2.0, like Windows NT server, is case-insensitive but case-preserving.

- Names in the user= list that begin with an at sign (@) expand to a list of users in the group of the same name.

Interoperability in More Detail

Sharing a Linux printer with Windows machines:

- Be sure that whatever path you define for a specific printer matches that defined for it in /etc/printcap.

The lines:

```
printcap name = /etc/printcap
load printers = yes
```

control the default loading of all printer definitions stored in /etc/printcap. Should your smb.conf contain these lines, you need not set up printers individually.

Sharing a Windows drive with Linux machines:

- Remember, when you run commands from a Linux box, that you may need to escape, that is, cause to be passed over rather than executed, some characters which Linux views as metacharacters with special meaning. So, for instance, the command

  ```
  /usr/sbin/smbclient \\sharedstuf\public a_password
  ```

  while syntactically correct from the Windows server's point of view, would have to be rendered as

  ```
  /usr/sbin/smbclient \\\\sharedstuf\\public
  a_password
  ```

  in order to cause Intel Unix to ignore, rather than carry out the symbolic function of, the backslash.

Browsing:

- Since browse lists are essentially a collection of broadcast messages that repeat at intervals of about 15 minutes, establishing a reliable browse list may require as much as 45 minutes, especially if that list must span network segments.

- The term domain master browser as used in this context refers, not to a Windows NT Domain, but rather to the master controller for browse list information. This being the case, WINS can play this role only in workgroups, and not across NT domains.

Protocols:

- Installing more than one protocol on a Windows machine very often results in browsing problems. Stick to TCP/IP.

- As one commentator on the topic puts it, in order for dhcpd to work correctly with picky DHCP clients such as Windows 95, it must be able to send packets with an IP destination address of 255.255.255.255. Most versions of Linux, however, will by default substitute the local subnet broadcast address. As a result, a DHCP protocol violation occurs, which, while it may be ignored by many clients, will cause some, such as Windows 95, to fail to see certain categories of messages from the DHCP server.

You can work around this problem under some Intel Unix versions by creating a route from the network interface address to 255.255.255.255. An example of a command which will accomplish this on most recent Linux distributions is:

```
route add -host 255.255.255.255 dev eth0
```

Troubleshooting in networked environments:

- Your smb.conf file may be located in /etc or in /usr/local/samba/lib.
- At the client end, ping can be run only from the DOS command line.
- ping can sometimes fail even when your TCP/IP installation is impeccable. If your Samba server is behind a firewall, that application's configuration may need to be relaxed.
- The most common reasons for a session request to be refused involve one or more of the following sample smb.conf entries:

```
hosts deny = ALL
hosts allow = 123.45.678.09/24
bind interfaces only = Yes
```

In these sample lines, no provision has been made for session requests that translate to the loopback address 127.0.0.1. Solve this problem by changing these lines as indicated below.

```
hosts deny = ALL
hosts allow = 123.45.678.09/24 127
```

- Having something already running on port 139 when a Samba server expects to use that port for the smbd daemon can also cause this type of error. To determine if this might happen in your environment, check your Internet daemon configuration file inetd.conf before trying to start smbd as a daemon.

Cautions Summary

We address only two topics in this section.

Advanced compilation and configuration:

- The native Windows versions of COMM don't work with applications running under WINE.
- WINE cannot work with the native Windows version of the ddraw DLL; that version is too heavily hardware-based to allow WINE to do so.
- The native version of the dinput DLL doesn't work with WINE.
- The dsound DLL's native version doesn't work with WINE.
- The keyboard DLL's native version doesn't work with WINE.
- There is no native Windows version of the WINEPS DLL; this DLL's name stands for WINE PostScript, and is the suite's builtin PostScript printer engine.

Troubleshooting in networked environments:

- nmbd does not support all WINS operations.

Appendix D

ECMA-234 and WinAPI Summary

In order to understand fully the problems WINE must address, one must understand the underpinnings of the interface WINE re-implements: the Microsoft APIs. This summary describes

- the ECMA-234 standard against which much of the Win32 API was designed
- the API itself

The ECMA-234 Standard

The ECMA-234 Standard is designed to define an environment in which

- applications written to its baseline will be highly portable
- the interface can react to open standards processes to meet current and future user needs in a timely fashion

ECMA-234 relies on current C language binding and encourages coding practices that will ensure that applications will conform to this standard. Further, it defines a set of application-programming interfaces that allow for the creation of graphical applications spanning a wide range of capabilities. The standard groups these APIs into major functional areas, including

- window manager interface
- graphics device interface

- interfaces needed to access system resources and capabilities

ECMA-234 focuses on providing the necessary APIs for writing applications for the desktop and also allows additional APIs to be bound to an application. This feature allows services such as database, networking, or other system services to be made available to applications.

In addition, ECMA-234 defines basic GUI objects such as buttons, scrollbars, menus, static and edit controls, and the painting functions needed to draw them, such as area fill, and line and rectangle drawing. Finally, a rich set of text routines is defined, from simple text output to more complex text output routines using multiple fonts and font styles, all supporting the use of color.

Anyone charged with understanding, implementing, and maintaining WINE should pay particular attention to the specifications for base services functions defined in ECMA-234. These base services give applications access to system and operating system resources such as memory, file systems, devices, processes, and threads. An application must use these functions to manage and monitor the resources it needs to complete its work. The remainder of this section briefly describes the several categories of such functions.

Process Management and Synchronization

Functions in this category start and coordinate the operation of multiple applications or multiple threads of execution within a single application.

File I/O

File I/O functions provide access to files, directories, and input and output (I/O) devices. These functions give applications access to files and directories on disks and other storage devices, whether on a specified computer or across a network. File I/O functions support a variety of file systems, including the FAT file system, the CD-ROM file system (CDFS), and NTFS.

Communications

Communications functions read from and write to communications ports. In addition, they control the operating modes of these ports. A subset within this category, called interprocess communication or IPC functions, includes DDE, pipe, mailslot, and file mapping functions.

Registry and Initialization

Functions in this category let applications store application-specific information in system files so that new invocations of the application or even other applications can retrieve and use the information.

Win32 Application Programming Interface

This section outlines the nature, structure, and shortcomings of the 32-bit Windows API, taking into account the standards set by ECMA-234.

Overview

Current versions of Windows rest on a 32-bit core Application Programming Interface (API) that covers an extremely broad range of categories. Table D-1 summarizes these API categories and the specific system resources they affect.

Table D-1 *Win32 API Categories*

Category	Affects
graphical elements	bitmaps, fonts, drawing primitives, area management functions, and 3D graphics
input and output devices	mouse, keyboard, pen, screen, printer, and sound
system services	files, memory, hardware, system databases, and networking
user interface	windows, menus, dialogs, input widgets, the clipboard, and internationalization functions

Other APIs must be used if an application is to satisfy Microsoft's licensing requirements for the *Designed for Windows NT and Windows 95 Logo Program.* These APIs include the following areas:

- Application automation and ActiveX
- Game applications (DirectX 2)
- Internet networking
- Messaging (MAPI)
- Microsoft's Component Object Model (COM)
- Object Linking and Embedding (OLE)
- Remote access services and procedure calls (RPC)
- Shell interfacing
- Telephony interfaces (TAPI)
- W3 server interfacing (Winsock, ISAPI)

The Win32 APIs also document interfaces for other, more recent, and less frequently implemented entities such as

- clustering
- management console
- Microsoft SQL Server
- Microsoft Transaction Server
- Micrsoft Exchange Server
- Open Database Connectivity Interface (ODBC)

Despite the APIs' reliance on C language bindings, its implementation as a set of shared libraries callable through conventions available to other languages makes it accessible from other languages and programming environments.

Finally, many scholars in the field consider the Win32 API

- difficult to master and use effectively
- not conducive to the safety, robustness, and portability of applications developed under it

Size, Structure, and Implementation

Programmers like the members of the WINE Project must access the Win32 API through a very large and complicated set of elements, whose true extent remains unclear. The Windows Software Development Kit (SDK) definition and contents change frequently. For example:

- The October 1996 edition of the Microsoft Development Library documents the Internet Server API (ISAPI) as part of the Win32 SDK, but documents other server-related APIs such as the Open Database Connectivity or ODBC API as separate entities.

- The April 1997 version of the Microsoft Development Library documents all Windows interfaces under the single banner PlatformSDK.

Most students of the topic consider the Win32 API

- to consist of the items supplied as parts of Microsoft's Win32 SDK
- to exclude the POSIX subsystem of Windows NT

Documentation supplied with the Win32 SDK lists 9,067 API elements, including functions, interface methods, structures, messages, macros, properties, and more. This number, however, does *not* include about 29,000 constants defined by means of the *#define* mechanism of the C preprocessor, and about 4,800 type definitions scattered throughout C header files within the SDK. Nor does the number 9,067 include the Unicode, ASCII, and character set neutral function forms. Table D-2 presents some key statistics regarding the Win32 API.

Table D-2 *Win32 API Statistics*

Element	Number
root header files	129
import libraries	48
general header files	232
aggregate header file size	5.2MB
aggregate number, non-empty and non-comment header file lines	120516
macro and constant definitions	33174

Continued

Table D-2 *Continued*

Element	Number
type definitions	4858
functions	3433
interface methods	1462
messages	858
structures	1077
properties	498
enumeration types	110
function error codes	1137

Such numbers and the constantly evolving nature of the Win32 API bring the challenge faced by the WINE Project clearly into focus: the difficulty of providing the same services on different platforms. The size, complexity, inconsistency, and constant evolution of the API make ensuring the correctness of programs using it an extremely difficult task. These factors also have important cost and interoperability consequences.

The structure of the Win32 API presents another problem: its reliance on a shared library, the Windows Dynamic Linked Libraries or DLLs. Current implementation of the API and its binding mechanism provide no version or interfacing control over applications using DLLs. Although DLLs can be associated with a version number, at a given time only a single version of a DLL can be loaded on the system. As a result major library interface changes, such as the transition to 32-bit code, rely on a haphazard mixture of simple renaming and replacing of library modules in order to satisfy new linkage requirements. This mixed approach, together with the monolithic structure and large size of the API, contribute to name-space problems. Any non-trivial Windows application must include the windows.h header file, which itself includes more than 60 other header files containing a total of more than 70,000 lines of C declarations and macro definitions.

Interface

Despite the surface generality of Win32 functions like CreateFile, no one should conclude that the Win32 API provides a single set of generalized functions that can handle a wide variety of tasks by being combined in an orthogonal fashion. Instead, Win32 provides 91 functions that create entities. These functions receive parameters of different types in greatly different orders. In addition, Win32 functions that create entities do not handle return values consistently. Table D-3 summarizes some of the latter type of problems.

Table D-3 *Returns from Functions Creating Entities*

Function	Returns
CreateFile	a handle to the file object on success and the INVALID_HANDLE_VALUE constant on error
CreateFileMapping	a handle to the mapping object on success and NULL on error
CreateHalftonePalette	a handle to the palette object on success and zero on error
CreatePipe	TRUE on success and FALSE on error
CreateTapePartition	NO_ERROR on success and any one of 15 constants on error

In addition to these complexities, 1,226 functions exist in three flavors relating to the character set they support:

- ANSI, an 8-bit superset of the ASCII character set
- Character set neutral
- Unicode

Unicode and ANSI versions of functions are named by appending the letter U or A respectively to the function name. Character set neutral functions are defined as C preprocessor macros that call one of the other two types of functions depending on source code compilation specifications.

Data Type-Related Problems

While the current ANSI C specifications provide a system of data types that aids in detecting type errors at compile time, the Win32 API provides, as one scholar notes, numerous possibilities for errors due to poorly specified arguments.

Other type-related problems exist. More than 150 functions pass an argument of the data type LPVOID or PVOID, that is, pointers to any data type. This technique effectively short-circuits a C compiler's type-checking system. The LPARAM and WPARAM entities constitute an even worse bending of data-typing rules. These simply specify 32-bit and 16-bit values respectively. Those values can then be used for any purpose, without type checks. Recent versions of the Win32 API contain

- 89 functions with an LPARAM argument
- 48 functions with a WPARAM argument

For example, the memory structure MSG structure, which houses message information, contains both an LPARAM and a WPARAM, each of which serves a different purpose for each of the 180 notification messages it helps to create and display.

Finally, Win32 API types extensively use the WORD and DWORD data types, defined respectively as 16- and 32-bit unsigned values, and most frequently used for passing flags and integer values. Such definition automatically limits the API's portability to future architectures with a different natural word size.

Function Names and Naming Conventions

The Win32 API uses inconsistent naming conventions. As a result, programmers often find its functions and constants hard to remember. In similar fashion, inconsistent capitalization can cause confusion. For example:

- Functions in the AVI group have names prefixed with uppercase letters
- Most functions in the media control interface or MCI group have names prefixed with lowercase letters
- Functions in the remote access service (RAS) group are prefixed with Ras

- Some functions inherited from other APIs (e.g., socket or string handling functions) have names made up entirely of lowercase characters

Finally, no consistent syntax exists for naming functions. As an example, consider the following functions, all of which relate to manipulating drawingbrushes.

- CreateSolidBrush
- FixBrushOrgEx
- GetBrushOrgEx

Portability

The Win32 API follows no established standard such as POSIX. In addition, even within the Windows family of OSes, significant barriers to portability exist. Of the 3433 readily available Win32 API functions

- 45 are not supported under Windows NT
- 602 are not supported under the earlier version of Windows 95
- 2,125 are not supported under Win32s, the set of drivers and library files for Windows 3.1 that upgrade them to provide a part of the 32-bit Windows API functionality

Table D-4 outlines the different levels of support for the Win32 API found in the various Microsoft operating systems.

Table D-4 *Win32 API Support in Microsoft OSes*

Windows Release	API Elements Introduced in Release
Windows NT 3.5	488
Windows 95	1,168
Windows NT 3.51	581
Windows NT 3.51 Service Pack 3	6
Windows NT 4.0	500
Windows NT 4.0 Service Pack 2	6
Windows NT 4.0 Service Pack 3	6
Windows NT 5.0 (proposed)	27

Functionality

The Win32 API provides inconsistent, inadequately documented, or incomplete functionality. These shortcomings directly affect the reliability of applications developed under it. Accessibility checking of memory addresses passed to functions demonstrates these flaws. Some functions check address accessibility and return an error if the addresses checked cannot be accessed. Others perform no such checking and can therfore cause the calling program to fail with the notorious *general protection fault* or GPF error when a bad address reaches the function.

The Win32 API's error handling in particular causes a variety of problems. Some functions clear a thread's global error code variable when they succeed; others do not. Most functions' documentation incompletely defines which of the 1,130 errors can occur in a call to that function, thereby making it nearly impossible to anticipate errors, and recover from them gracefully.

Some functions offer only very rudimentary, low-level functionality, thereby imposing on applications a workload that should have been covered by the operating system. Others, such as the video capture API, provide higher-level, but still incomplete, functionality. For example, setting the video source by means of a dialog box displayed to the user by calling the capDlgVideoSource function cannot be done from within an application.

The Win32 API follows an event processing model. Applications have to continuously process events posted by the operating system in order to exhibit the liveness properties the OS expects, and to comply with the provided interface. This event model conflicts with several application designs, algorithms, legacy applications, and system requirement specifications. However, other models for asynchronous operation have to be used in combination with the event processing model. These combinations present numerous opportunities for programming that can result in deadlocks. Some examples are as follows:

- Calling the Win32 API while holding a level 3 or device-level lock
- Creating windows and calling the Sleep function with an inappropriate delay
- Failing to acknowledge an incoming dynamic data exchange DDE request
- Sending a message to a thread that yields control after receiving the message

Suggested Remedies

The scholars upon whose work this summary relies suggest a specific treatment for the problems this section describes. That treatment turns out also to describe WINE accurately, and includes

- using programming languages and libraries to isolate applications from the Win32 API's specific characterisitics
- providing well-designed, generic, high-level functionality for accomplishing Windows-like tasks

Index

Continued

Continued

my2cents.idgbooks.com